MAKE THAT GRADE
LAND LAW

Jack Anderson

GILL & MACMILLAN

Gill & Macmillan Ltd
Hume Avenue
Park West
Dublin 12
with associated companies throughout the world
www.gillmacmillan.ie

© 2002 Jack Anderson
0 7171 3340 0

Print origination by O'K Graphic Design, Dublin

*The paper used in this book is made from the wood pulp of managed forests.
For every tree felled, at least one tree is planted, thereby renewing natural resources.*

A catalogue record is available for this book from the British Library.

CONTENTS

Note to the text: For convenience, the male gender has been used throughout the text, though male and/or female gender is implied as appropriate.

INTRODUCTION

Prior to the Industrial Revolution land was the primary source of wealth. Land, and the control of land, led to power, influence and dominance. Land law is concerned with the rights and liabilities that arise under our law in respect of land. Traditionally, land law was designed to secure title, though later it expanded to promote the greater marketability of land as a commodity.

Land in this context includes more than just rock and soil. The legal definition of land includes all permanent structures attached to the land, such as buildings and other 'things', which can be deemed permanently attached to the land. For example, apart from buildings, things such as fence posts and gates are treated as land. Partly for this reason, this area of the law is often known as the law of *real property* where 'real' derives from the Latin word *res* meaning 'thing'. This broad definition of 'land' and its permanent attachments is reflected in Paragraph 14 of the Schedule to the Interpretation Act 1937.

All other property comprising movables, such as furniture, is deemed personal property or *personalty*. In medieval times the most important moveable asset was stock, usually cattle; hence, *chattels* came to be used to describe anything that fell under the heading of personalty.

In the past, there were some fundamental differences between real and personal property, particularly as regards succession rights. For example, originally only personal property could be disposed of on death by will; later *realty* could be disposed of under a will. However, a distinction between realty and personalty remained in the absence of a will. Realty passed to the heir in accordance with the ancient rules of descent, whereas personalty was divided among the surviving next of kin. Under the Succession Act 1965, provisions were introduced that assimilated the rules for the distribution of real and personal property on death. In an overall sense, the demarcation between what is real and what is personal property is now largely irrelevant under Irish law.

Land law's primary concern is that of ownership. The ancient maxim *Nulle terre sans seigneur* (no land without master) is still as potent as ever. Furthermore, under our classic definition of land law, land cannot be owned directly by anyone; rather, one has an interest, an estate or a right in land and these interests, estates and rights together constitute ownership.

Accordingly, when faced with almost any issue under Irish land law, students must confront three fundamental issues:

1. the need to establish the various parties who claim to have rights, interests or estates in the land in question
2. the need to define these rights
3. the need to examine the extent to which these rights can be enjoyed, if at all, by the parties in question.

Thus, land law is concerned with a wide variety of estates and interests that may exist in land and with the various methods of regulating and utilising these rights. These difficulties are exacerbated by the fact that the supply of land is finite. Where something is finite, its exploitation will inevitably be controversial and land, as private property, is no different in this regard. In any transaction involving land, the complications faced by the lawyer may be acute, ranging from tracing the original title; to ascertaining the present rights of the current owner; to identifying future interests that may restrict the use of the land. These are difficult tasks.

This text attempts to demystify and rationalise these problems for students of Irish land law (regrettably, given the limited size of this text, certain general issues, such as family property, and certain individual issues, such as treasure trove, cannot be dealt with) and is designed in a 'student friendly' manner. Each chapter follows a specific, thematic approach. For example, Chapter 1 explains that, unlike other areas of Irish law, land law in Ireland has many unique and indigenous characteristics. Therefore from a practical point of view, comparative English texts on land law must be used with caution, given that they do not always reflect even the most basic of Irish principles.

Each of the 10 chapters concludes with 'self-test' questions. Some of these take the form of straightforward, discursive essay questions while others are based on factual problems. Both types of question will assist students' preparation for examination. Finally, apart from references to case law within the text, suggestions for further reading, largely taken from the following texts, are also given at the end of each chapter.

Reference texts

Coughlan, P., *Property Law*, 2nd edn. Dublin: Gill & MacMillan, 1998.
Lyall, A., *Land Law in Ireland*, 2nd edn. Dublin: Round Hall Sweet & Maxwell, 2000.
Pearce, R.A. and Mee, J, *Land Law*, 2nd edn. Dublin: Sweet & Maxwell, 2000.
Wylie, J., *A Casebook on Irish Land Law*, Oxford: Professional Books Limited, 1984.
Wylie, J., *Irish Land Law*, 3rd edn. Dublin: Butterworths, 1997.

1
HISTORICAL BACKGROUND

Irish land law is a difficult subject. Basic principles are often complicated, even archaic. One of the reasons for this complexity is that Irish land law reflects, in a general sense, the history of the Irish nation. This history is largely a colonial experience, wherein land, and the control of land, was crucial. The plantations of the seventeenth century, the subsequent penal laws, the famine, Davitt and Parnell's campaigns for land reform and ultimately the land purchasing schemes of the late nineteenth century, are as fundamental to modern Irish land law as they are to our general history.

Paradoxically, this peculiar historical experience has led many Irish jurists to remark that of all branches of law, land law has resisted most the domineering influence of English common law. In short, Irish land law has, particularly in the area of landlord and tenant law, retained many idiosyncratic 'Irish' characteristics. This theme will run throughout this text and it is an important one to remember. From a practical point of view it means that comparative English texts on land law must be treated with caution, as they do not always reflect nor even share the most basic of principles.

The historical background to Irish land law can be divided into five subsections:

- the pre-twelfth century era as dominated by Brehon law principles
- the period between the twelfth century and the seventeenth century, wherein Ireland became the 'first adventure of the common law'
- the plantation of Ireland by the Tudor monarchies, entailing the confiscation of large amounts of land held under native title
- the campaign for land reform in the post-famine era and the legislative reaction of the Westminster authorities in the form of land purchasing schemes
- developments in land law since the foundation of the State, an era that is marked by greater public regulation of land, for example, in the form of the planning laws.

Brehon law

Brehon law was largely a custom-based system which served a self-sufficient mixed-farming economy based on the raising of cattle, sheep, pigs and the growing of cereal. Thus, land and the control of land was vital to the organisation and security of this culture. Society was organised in tribes based on kin or family groups (*fine*) with the kin possessing ultimate legal control over its members. The kin elected a leader or chief (*Taoiseach*). In assuming power, the Taoiseach succeeded to the rights of the land and all the related property under his control in a process known as *tanistry*. This law of succession decreed that all land and other property connected with the chieftaincy would pass to the *tanist*, that is, the eldest and worthiest male kinsman of the current chief. This person was usually chosen in the lifetime of the chief in an attempt to ensure a smooth transition of power.

In a general sense, land was administered on a co-operative basis, wherein a process known as *gavelkind* governed succession to individual plots of land. Under this system, the youngest son divided the land into equal parts. Subsequently, the eldest son chose a plot for himself, then the second son, and so on until the youngest son took the last piece. Thus, it was in the youngest son's own interest to divide the land equally. The sophistication of the process lay in the fact that its equality did not depend on altruism; everyone acting in his own best interest achieved the equality.

The feudal system

In the 1170s the Norman conquest of Ireland began under King Henry II. In legal terms this entailed the introduction of common law — based on a feudal system — into Ireland. The feudal system was primarily a system of administration designed to centralise and secure the country under the authoritative power of the King. Critical to this objective was the administration of land, as governed by the concept of *tenure* under which all land was ultimately held and distributed by the King as chief lord superior, that is, lord paramount.

In Ireland, the common law's feudalism came into inevitable and well-documented conflict with existing native title. Herein lies the original and lingering distinction between English and Irish land tenure. In traditional English feudalism there was a certain element of co-operation and reciprocity in the land system — the lord led and administered the estate for the good of all and the tenants supplied rent, food and services, especially military services, to protect 'their' land. In Ireland, the system was largely imposed on a population unwilling to abandon their traditional kin-based system. Writing in 1881, Judge Longfield, a celebrated judge of the Landed Estates Courts in Ireland, summarised this hostility:

In both countries the law is based upon the feudal system, which gave the landlord a certain superiority over his tenant. But the feudal relation, with its reciprocal rights and duties, never existed in Ireland ... in a great part of Ireland sudden and violent transfer of the lordship was often made to persons whom the tenant only knew as their victorious enemy.

Plantations and penal laws

This 'violent transfer' took place largely during the sixteenth and seventeenth centuries when a comprehensive confiscation and resettlement of land occurred in Ireland — the plantations. The administration of King Henry VIII pursued a policy of 'surrender and re-grant'. Under this scheme the chief Irish landowners were induced to enter into a formal agreement with the Crown whereby they submitted to English feudal law, surrendered their lands and obtained in return a re-grant of that land to be held in accordance with feudal principles of ultimate loyalty to the King. If they refused, their land was forcibly taken off them or *escheated* under so-called Acts of Attainder and resettled with outsiders or planters.

In parallel with this policy, the common law courts attacked Brehon law concepts such as tanistry and gavelkind because the continuation of Brehon law principles was inherent in their element of succession; see further the case of *Gavelkind* (1605) Dav 49 and the case of *Tanistry* (1607) Dav 28. Tanistry and gavelkind were to be replaced by the common law's system of *primogeniture* whereby land passed on all occasions to the eldest surviving male or in *coparcenary* where no males survived. In effect, these decisions, as linked to the further military conquest of Ireland in the seventeenth century, sounded the death knell of Brehon law as an influential body of law; see further *Moore* v *Attorney General* [1934] IR 44.

By the eighteenth century, many English landowners had acquired grants of large areas of Irish land but the agrarian disturbances in Ireland did little to entice them as owner-occupiers. They preferred to remain absentee landlords and to turn the running of their Irish estates over to agents. These middlemen had one abiding aim: to make as much profit out of the land by every means possible — the amount of commission they earned depended on this. The result was the widespread subdivision of these large estates. The subdivision was based on leaseholds. The leases were time-limited and had to be renewed on the death of the leaseholder. Therefore, not only was the agent earning a steady income for his master from the lease but he could also levy a fine for each renewal of the lease. The proliferation of various types of leases was encouraged by legislation — the so-called 'penal laws' — which imposed various discriminations on Catholics, in particular debarring them from purchasing land and limiting the length of lease they could hold. An example of this was an Irish Statute of 1703 2 Ann, c6 (Ir), which debarred Catholics from purchasing land and limited the length of a lease they could obtain to 31 years.

By the nineteenth century, the Irish tenant's legal and economic position was distressing. Estates became more and more subdivided into less and less economical units. Rent, which was already disproportionately steep, was usually paid in arrears, on a *gale day* — a day on which a periodic payment of rent is due. The threat of distress or eviction was constant. The tenant also had to meet the expense of the tithe — the right to one-tenth of the produce of the land in a parish, owed to the Church of Ireland, a Church to which the tenant may not even have belonged.

Moreover, the years 1817 to 1851 were a disaster for Irish agriculture, which had previously sustained itself by supplying both Britain and France with food during the Napoleonic Wars. Severe famine was experienced in Ireland in 1817, 1822 and most spectacularly of all in 1845–7. By the second half of the century the country was ripe for reform and renewed campaigns for reform in land law began in line with political developments for Home Rule. In 1879 Michael Davitt formed the Land League in Co. Mayo and this soon became a national movement, with Parnell as president.

Land reform

Westminster and in particular the liberal Prime Minister, Gladstone, took notice and in 1870 the Landlord and Tenant (Ireland) Act was passed. The Act gave limited statutory recognition throughout the island of Ireland to the so-called 'Ulster Custom'. This custom guaranteed the right of the tenant to remain in possession of the land so long as he paid his rent and fulfilled his obligations, with reasonable limits being placed on increases in rent for improvements made by the tenant. The custom also permitted the tenant to sell his interest without having to obtain the consent of the landlord. Finally, the custom gave the tenant the right to reasonable compensation on eviction, termination or other disturbance of the tenancy.

While the 1870 Act was welcome, it was somewhat limited in its application — it was literally an Ulster custom. Furthermore, the Act did not give Irish tenants the basic security of tenure they sought. Irish tenants did not want compensation after eviction; they wanted protection from eviction itself.

Further reform was needed and in 1881 a Land Act was passed guaranteeing the 'three Fs':

- fair rent
- free sale
- fixity of tenure.

The Act also established a Land Commission, which determined the three Fs in relation to each case. As regards fair rent, the tenant had the right to apply to the Commission to have a fair rent fixed. Once the court determined a price, the rent became legally binding. As regards free sale, tenants were also given the right to sell their interest in the land and objections by the landlord could be appealed to the Commission to determine the reasonableness of the objection. As regards fixity of tenure, the Act granted tenants a *judicial tenancy*, in effect a statutory term of 15 years. Thereafter, the tenancy was subject to review with the existing tenant retaining first option on any transaction. The 1881 Act was an initial success and a milestone in Irish land law. About three-quarters of the qualifying tenants took advantage of it and the Act seemed much more 'tenant-friendly' than previous legislation. Indeed, the first statutory adjustment of rents under the 1881 Act reduced rents by approximately 20 per cent on average.

Under Section 24 of the 1881 Act the Irish Land Commission agreed to advance three-quarters of the purchase price of the land in question to the tenant at low interest (5 per cent) with the annuities to be paid back over a long period of time (35 years or so). Indeed, under Section 26 of the Act, if a proportion of tenants on a particular estate were willing to buy their holdings, the Land Commission was given power to purchase the whole of that estate with a view to selling off parts to the tenants. Even more generous purchasing provisions were provided for under the Ashbourne Act 1885, the Balfour Acts of 1891 and 1896 and finally the Irish Land Act 1903 sponsored by George Wyndham, then Secretary of State for Ireland.

The modern era

The cumulative effects of these provisions were enormous and, by the 1920s, some 316,000 holdings comprising an area of about 11,000,000 acres of land had been bought throughout the island for a total price of about £100 million. Essentially, these land purchasing schemes formed the basis for much of modern Irish land law and the subsequent adoption of a written constitution evidently added a new dimension to the common law system of land law — nothing more so than Article 43 of *Bunreacht na hÉireann* in which there is an unequivocal recognition and guarantee of the right to the private ownership of property.

The concept of equity

While the impact of constitutional concerns on the common law's system of land law has been quite recent, the influence of the concept of equity has a much longer and invasive history.

In its early development the common law relied heavily on a procedure known as the *writ system*. In order for an action to be brought to the early common law courts, a writ appropriate to the cause of action had to be obtained. In this, the writ detailed the exact nature of the legal claim and its factual basis. Under the Statute of Westminster II 1285 the issuing of writs was effectively confined to varying the form of existing writs. In other words, unless your claim came within the form of a recognised writ, then it was a *wrong*, which may in common law, remain without remedy. Thus, the common law became rigid and static.

As a result of this defect, the practice of petitioning directly to the King developed. The King delegated these hearings to an officer called the Lord Chancellor whose administration became known as the Court of Chancery and whose principles became known as *equity*. In the Court of Chancery, the basic procedure was that the plaintiff raised his complaint by presenting a petition or bill to the Chancellor. If the court thought there was a case to answer it would issue a *subpoena* ('under pain') ordering the defendant to appear and answer the complaint. A defendant who failed to observe a decree of the Chancellor could be imprisoned for contempt of court. In addition, this independent Court of Chancery took a less rigid and more balanced approach to justice than the common law courts and to this effect created a number of legal features unknown to the common law. Some of these features play an important role in land law.

At this stage it is important to note that equity is not a 'stand alone' legal system, its principles are not first principles; one has to show that one has not initially received justice at common law. Equity does not supplant the law but supplements it; it recognises and enforces the rights and duties of which the common law takes no notice. The two do not clash; rather, one takes up where the other leaves off. As Maitland — one of the great jurists of equity — stated:

> Equity comes not to destroy the law but to fulfil it.

The underlying concern of the innovative equitable interventions of the Court of Chancery was said to be the prevention of unconscionable conduct. Given the nature of this task, the original Chancellors were invariably clerics, who based their decision on the flexible notion of what was 'just and equitable' given the circumstances of the case. By the seventeenth century, the

Court of Chancery had firmly established itself as an independent system of justice. Indeed, many of its remedies, such as injunctions and decrees of specific performance, overshadowed and even curtailed the operation of the common law, which remained reliant on the remedy of damages.

To this end, a conflict between the courts was inevitable. Matters came to a head in the early seventeenth century when the Chief Justice of England, Edward Coke, disputed the jurisdiction of the Court of Chancery to restrain actions at common law and held in a number of cases that imprisonment for disobeying injunctions was unlawful. In short, Coke was arguing that equity was no longer supplementing the law but subverting it. The Lord Chancellor, Lord Ellesmere, rejected the argument and claimed that he was simply controlling the way legal rights were exercised in the interest of justice in particular individual cases. The issue finally had to be confronted by King James I in the case of the *Earl of Oxford* (1615).

The result of the case was favourable to the development of equity. Thereafter, the consolidation of the status of equity was also assisted by the fact that by the mid-seventeenth century the Chancellors were generally common law lawyers rather than members of the clergy (the last of the non-legal Chancellors was Lord Shaftesbury who held office from 1672–3). Gradually, these legally trained Chancellors began to base their equitable discretion not according to their 'conscience' but according to precedent. It was with Shaftesbury's successor, Lord Nottingham (1673–82), often referred to as the father of modern equity, that the development of a settled system of equity began in earnest.

This development was continued by Lord Hardwicke (1736–56) and the great Lord Eldon (1801–6 and 1807–27). However, by the nineteenth century, the bureaucracy, corruption and delays in the system's administrative structure were stunting the development of equity. For example, until 1813 there were only two judges in the Court of Chancery, the Lord Chancellor and the Master of the Rolls, who started life as the Lord Chancellor's assistant, eventually evolving into an independent judge. In addition to such staff shortages the workings of the court itself were anachronistic and cumbersome. All evidence had to be forwarded by an affidavit and, most absurdly of all, if you sought to claim a remedy in one court, for example, in a common law court like Common Pleas or the Queen's Bench, you could not seek that remedy in the Court of Chancery, so your case could float between the two systems for a considerable length of time.

The nineteenth century did, however, see much reform in the area. In 1854 in England the Common Law Procedure (Amendment) Act was passed, which gave the common law courts the power to grant equitable remedies in limited situations (enacted in Ireland in 1856). In 1858 the Chancery (Amendment) Act (often called Lord Cairn's Act) gave the Court of Chancery the power to award the common law remedy of damages either in substitution for or in addition to an injunction. However, the major change came with the Judicature Acts — the Supreme Court of Judicature Acts 1873 and 1875, followed in Ireland by the Supreme Court of Judicature (Ireland) Act 1877. These Acts were to have a fundamental and defining effect on the relationship between the law and equity; a debate that continues to this day. The 1877 Act declared that thereafter there would be one Supreme Court of Judicature only, consisting of a High Court and a Court of Appeal, and that the principles of law and equity were to be applied in every case.

It must be noted, however, that the Judicature Acts fused only the administration of the common law and equity; they did not fuse their principles and it remains the case that the equitable jurisdiction can and does make a distinctive contribution to all major areas of the law; none more so than land law.

The influence of equity on land law

Though equity has contributed substantially to the law on mortgages and restrictive covenants, arguably its most important contribution to land law is the development of the concept of use, in which the origins of the modern concept of the trust lie. The scheme of a use is straightforward — a person holds property, not for his own benefit, but for the benefit of another; for example, the owner transfers property to A for the use of B. As will be demonstrated in this arrangement, A has legal title and B equitable title. There is a restriction on A's ownership of the property in that the property must be used by A for the benefit of B.

In one sense the origins of the concept of use are somewhat dramatic in that its development can be traced back to the Crusades — a knight going on crusade would transfer his property to a neighbour who would hold it for the benefit of the wife and children of the knight. The common law courts did not recognise this mechanism, thus, in our example, A (or the knight's neighbour) would be the properly constituted owner of the transferred property. However, the Courts of Chancery felt that it would be inequitable and unconscionable to allow the legal owner (traditionally called the *feoffee to uses*) to ignore the terms of the transfer and the rights of the beneficiaries, that is, B or the knight's wife and children (the beneficiaries or also the *cestuis que vie*).

With its recognition by the Courts of Chancery, the popularity of use increased and it was seen to be particularly helpful in facilitating the avoidance of certain feudal dues and incidents. It also facilitated the disposition of land under a will, as it was not until the Statute of Wills

(Ireland) Act 1634 that such a will could be made directly. Indeed, largely because it facilitated the avoidance of taxes, a Statute of Uses was passed in England in 1535 that attempted to abolish the concept. The aim of these provisions was to cause the legal title to be placed in the person in whose favour the use was created (the *cestui que use*); in our example (to A for the use of B), under the Statute, B now has equitable and legal title and A is left with nothing.

By the time this provision was enacted in Ireland in 1634 a number of issues had arisen in the application of the provision. First, the Statute applied only where the feoffee to use received freehold property and did not apply to leasehold property. In addition, the Statute was not applicable where the person to whom the freehold was transferred had an active duty to perform, for example, to collect rent. And finally, the scheme of the Act could be avoided by utilising the so-called 'use upon a use'.

In the case of *Tyrell* (1557), the common law courts in England were basically confronted with the following dilemma: how would the Statute of Uses deal with a transfer of land 'To A to the use of B to the use of C'? The common law courts interpreted the Statute as transferring A's legal title to the first-named beneficiary, B, with C receiving nothing. In effect, the common law courts held that the Statute of Uses could be applied only once and was then exhausted. This ruling was questioned increasingly by the Court of Chancery and, indeed, by the mid-seventeenth century it was settled that the 'use upon a use' would be recognised and enforced in equity, thereby creating the foundations of the modern trust.

It then became common to reduce 'To A to the use of B to the use of C' to 'Unto and to the use of B [the trustee] in trust for C [the beneficiary]'. In this we can locate the origins of the modern trust.

Priorities and the doctrine of notice

As is implicit from the above examples, the owner of land can create a variety of successive estates and interests (both legal and equitable) in his property so as to give various persons rights over that land. It follows that issues of priority may arise, that is, which of the estates or interests will the courts recognise and enforce?

It is established that where there are two competing legal interests the one which was created first prevails. Similarly, where there are two competing equitable interests in land, the maxim *Where the equities are equal the first in time prevails* is followed. Where a person purchases the legal estate of a property that is the subject of a trust — an equitable interest — it is generally held that if the purchaser is aware, at the time of acquisition, of the existence of the trust he is 'in good conscience' bound by the equitable interest. However, the purchaser of the legal estate is entitled to take the property free of equitable rights if he can show that he was a 'bona fide purchaser of the legal estate for value without notice'.

The person entitled to this exemption is often described as 'equity's darling', though the purchaser must clearly satisfy all aspects of the exemption before availing of it. First, the term *bona fide* ('in good faith') is related partly to the definition of notice but it is also indicative of the fact that any fraud on the part of the purchaser would deprive him of priority; see *Midland Bank Trust v Green* [1981] AC 513, where there was evidence that the purchaser was in collusion with another to defeat the equitable rights of others. Second, as we saw earlier, equity supplements the common law and does not supplant it, a concept which is neatly expressed in the maxim *Equity follows the law*. In determining priorities, courts will always recognise the superior status attributed to the legal interest as against the equitable interest. In this instance, the maxim translates to the effect that in order to obtain priority over an existing equitable estate or interest the purchaser would have to acquire a legal estate or interest. Third, the purchaser must acquire the property at value, that is, adequate consideration must have been provided. And finally, the purchaser of the legal title will obtain priority over a prior equitable estate or interest only if he purchased without notice of it.

Section 3(1) of the Conveyancing Act 1882 states the elements of notice. Essentially there are three types:

- actual
- constructive
- imputed.

In actual notice, the purchaser knows as a matter of fact of the right in question. If the purchaser has heard only vague rumours, this does not amount to actual notice; see further *O'Connor v McCarthy* [1982] IR 161. In many ways, constructive notice is an application of *caveat emptor* ('let the buyer beware') in that the purchaser is obliged to take all reasonable steps to investigate the existence of any other applicable equitable rights. For example, the physical state of the land may indicate the likelihood of an equitable right inconsistent with the interest that the vendor has agreed to sell. Furthermore, if there is an occupier on the land, the purchaser must enquire what that person's rights are; see further *Hunt v Luck* [1901] Ch 45. Indeed, a purchaser is bound by the rights of any occupant of the land of whom he made no enquiry; see further Kenny, J., in *Northern Bank Ltd v Henry* [1981] IR 1. Imputed notice is the actual or constructive notice of an agent employed for the transaction, for example, a solicitor employed to do the conveyancing.

It must be noted that where land is registered, as most agricultural land in Ireland is, the statutory provisions of the Registration of Title Act 1964 apply and the equitable doctrine of notice is largely excluded. Application of the doctrine of notice may also be avoided by reference to the Registration of Deeds Act (Ireland) 1707. The relationship between priority and these registration mechanisms is further discussed in Chapter 7.

Further reading

Historical background

Byrne, R. and McCutcheon, J.P., *Irish Legal System*, 3rd edn. Dublin: Butterworth, 1996, Chapter 2.

Wylie, J., *Irish Land Law*, 3rd edn. Dublin: Butterworths, 1997, Chapter 1.

Wylie, J., *A Casebook on Irish Land Law*, Oxford: Professional Books Limited, 1984, pp. 1–40.

Equity

Coughlan, P., *Property Law*, 2nd edn. Dublin: Gill & MacMillan, 1998, Chapters 4 and 5.

Wylie, J., *A Casebook on Irish Land Law*, Oxford: Professional Books Limited, 1984, pp. 67–112.

Wylie, J., *Irish Land Law*, 3rd edn. Dublin: Butterworths, 1997, Chapter 3.

Self-test

Ireland was the 'first adventure of the common law' but the importation of the common law into Ireland was not a seamless one.

Is this statement particularly true of Irish land law?

2
TENURE

In feudal times, the terms, manner or condition under which land was held was known as tenure. This tenure was based largely on services owed to the owner. Non-performance of these services could lead to forfeiture.

Under classic feudal law, all land belonged ultimately to the King who, having the power to allocate land, could consequently secure the financial and military support of his subjects. Unsurprisingly, the initial grants of land made by the Norman Kings were awarded to their closest followers and supporters who had assisted in the conquest of territory; for example, the first grant in Ireland was of the ancient Irish kingdom of Leinster, awarded to Richard de Clare ('Strongbow') by King Henry II, in 1171.

Land was held by each grantee under the King, subject to terms and conditions of tenure. In turn, the grantee usually sub-granted parts of the land. This process of subdividing the land was called *subinfeudation*. Thus a pyramidal, hierarchical structure of land ownership — apexed by the King — was created and bound together by the principle of tenure. Under this system, all land was said to be holden of some lord, save the King's own private land, which could not be holden of any superior. It was said that the King, as lord paramount, held his own land in *allodial*.

Thus, at the top of this pyramid of interests and held in absolute ownership were the King's private lands, the *royal demesne*. The initial grant of land was then awarded to the King's immediate subordinates — the *tenants in chief*. They might in turn sub-grant land to *mesne tenants*, so called because they occupied the intermediate tiers of the pyramid. Below this were the *tenants in demesne* and finally within the foundations of the pyramid could be found the *villeins*, known in Ireland as *betaghs*. These villeins or betaghs had little legal status. When not required to work for the lord of the manor they would typically cultivate their own subsistence crops.

In theory, the great benefit of this structure was that it engendered security and unity, with everyone, bar the King, sharing the common experience of being under an obligation to those higher up in the pyramid. However, the reality was quite different and feudal society was unquestionably hierarchical and discriminatory in nature.

This inequality is clearly demonstrated by the fact that the obligations or conditions of tenure differed immensely depending on the classification of tenure and also on the tenant's location within the pyramid. Essentially, there were two types of tenure: free and unfree. In free tenure, the emphasis was on the rights of the tenants, and limits were set on the extent of services they had to perform. Typically, free tenants had an implicit right to quiet enjoyment of their land and could bring actions in the King's courts. In contrast, unfree tenants had few rights but plenty of obligations.

There were three major types of free tenure:

- military tenure, which was linked with the provision of military services
- *frankalmoign* (literally 'free alms'), which concerned ecclesiastical land, that is, land held by monasteries and convents. The motives for a local lord to make a grant of frankalmoign were both religious — in return for the tenure the religious order would pray for the lord's soul — and economic — income from the land would be used by the Church to provide for the poor. As a result of this type of tenure, the Church became an extensive and influential landowner during the feudal era.
- tenure in socage, by far the most prevalent type of free tenure, in which the tenure was based around agricultural obligations, that is, cultivating the land.

Free tenants had a certain legal interest in the land, known as *seisin* — the right to freehold possession of the land. Free tenants were said to 'seise' the land subject to the obligations of tenure, whereas unfree tenants had no such interest or seisin in the land. The principal category of unfree tenure was *villeinage* in which villeins, or betaghs, were legally bound to the manor in which they lived. In England, a customary law — *copyhold* — developed to protect the rights of villeins; see *Pigg* v *Caley* (1618) Noy's Reports 27, 74 ER 997. However, this type of tenure — 'tenure by copy of the court roll' — did not transfer to Ireland.

The obligations of each tenure were broken down, in a technical sense, into various services and incidents owed to the immediate lord but collectively these services and incidents were known as *seigniory* — the collection of rights enjoyed by the feudal lord. The extent of services and incidents owed varied depending on the type of tenure in question. Typical incidents included fealty, which was a personal oath of allegiance to the immediate lord; wardship, whereby the immediate lord had the right to manage the land of an infant heir of one of his tenants; relief and aid, which were land taxes levied by the King or the immediate lord; and finally escheat, whereby land would revert back to the immediate lord if the tenant breached the obligations of tenure.

With the passing of time, many obligations were simply commuted to money payments, sometimes called *scutage*, and eventually, through the effects of inflation, the payments were rendered a nominal commitment only. This was one of the reasons for the demise of the feudal system of tenure, of which little survives today. Moreover, this demise was assisted by statutory reform: Magna Carta in 1215 limited the arbitrary power of the King to raise taxes from the land; Quia Emptores in 1290 attempted to regulate the process of subinfeudation; and finally the Tenure Abolition Act of 1660 (Ireland, 1662) essentially promoted one type of agricultural tenure — free and common *socage* or, in modern terms, *freehold*.

Further reading

Coughlan, P., *Property Law*, 2nd edn. Dublin: Gill & MacMillan, 1998, Chapter 2.
Lyall, A., *Land Law in Ireland*, 2nd edn. Dublin: Round Hall Sweet & Maxwell, 2000, Chapter 3.
Wylie, J., *Irish Land Law*, 3rd edn. Dublin: Butterworths, 1997, Chapter 2.

Self-test

In *Mabo* v *Queensland* (No. 2) (1993) 1 LRC 194, the High Court of Australia held, for the first time, that the common law of Australia recognised the antecedent land rights of the Aboriginal people.

In the light of your understanding of the feudal concept of tenure, discuss the merits of Brennan, J.'s judgement in *Mabo* and the manner in which he reconciles native title with common law principles.

3
ESTATES

Tenure can be defined as the terms and conditions under which land was held in feudal times. The duration of this interest in the land was defined by the concept of estates. There are two principal categories of estates — freehold and leasehold — though there are also certain hybrid estates, which have characteristics of both.

Initially, the life estate was the only freehold estate recognised at common law. Where land was granted in the traditional feudal manner between lord and tenant, the life of the tenant constituted the maximum duration of the tenant's interest because the grant had been made on the basis that the tenant would personally render services, incidents and allegiance to the lord. Given the strict personal nature of this arrangement, the estate ended automatically on the death of the tenant; thus, the tenant's interest in the land became known as the *life estate*.

Over the course of time, tenants sought and earned greater security of tenure and developed greater powers to deal with the land. This increasing freedom of alienability, which was given statutory recognition by Quia Emptores in 1290, was accompanied by the development of a new and elongated type of freehold estate — the *fee simple*. The fee simple amounted to an interest in land that could last longer than the life of the initial tenant and had the potential to last forever. In modern terms, the fee simple is regarded as the nearest the common law comes to a concept of absolute ownership allied to complete alienability.

The freedom of alienability inherent in the fee simple was advantageous in that it ensured that land remained a marketable and transferable commodity. Yet, in medieval times this flexibility was viewed with a certain amount of suspicion. Land was the ultimate source of power and influence in this society and medieval landowners were anxious to ensure that the family lands remained in the family name from one generation to the next. Thus, the practice of cutting down the fee simple estate in a manner that limited the estate to a narrow class of direct heirs developed. This type of limited freehold estate is known as the *fee tail*.

Estate creation and words of limitation

The proper creation of the various estates requires that the appropriate words of limitation be used.

In general, any basic transaction involving a freehold estate can be divided into two parts. First, thère are the *words of limitation*, which are the words delimiting or defining the estate being conveyed. These words are to be distinguished from the *words of purchase*, which indicate the person to whom the estate is being conveyed. For example, in the disposition of land 'To A in fee simple', the words 'To A' are the words of purchase and the words 'in fee simple' are the words of limitation.

The equation differs depending on the type of freehold estate in question, that is, different words of limitation must be used to create a fee simple, a fee tail or a life estate. The words of limitation vary depending on whether the transaction occurs *inter vivos*, as in between living persons, or, in a will. If the incorrect words of limitation are used, a life estate only is disposed.

The adherence to this strict approach has been justified on the grounds that it brings certainty to the ownership and transfer of land; see further *Re Coleman's Estate* [1907] 1 IR 488 and *Re Adam's Estate* [1965] IR 57.

Fee simples inter vivos

At common law, the proper words of limitation appropriate to the creation of a fee simple inter vivos were 'and his heirs', for example, 'To A and his heirs'. Section 51 of the Conveyancing Act 1881 permits the use of the formula 'in fee simple' as an alternative. Both constructions are interpreted strictly by the courts; see further *Re Ford and Ferguson's Contract* [1906] 1 IR 607 where the expression 'To A in fee' was deemed to give A a life estate only.

Fee simples by will

The courts take a more liberal interpretation to the interpretation of wills. Prior to 1838 a will had only to demonstrate that there was an intention to create a fee simple. Thus, a formula such as 'To A for ever' or 'To A absolutely', created a fee simple. Under Sections 28 and 34 of the Wills Act 1837, the fee simple, or other whole interest of which the testator had power to dispose, passed to the grantee. This presumption is repeated in Section 94 of the Succession Act 1965. Section 94 also repeats the proviso that this presumption can be rebutted if a contrary intention appears from the will; see further *Re Gannon* [1914] 1 IR 86.

Modified fee simples

The grantor may modify the basic or absolute fee simple. The creation of modified fee simples utilises similar terminology to the creation of an absolute fee simple except that it may contain a determinable or conditional factor.

A determinable fee simple is a fee simple that will terminate automatically on the occurrence of the stated event. It is not certain that the event in question will occur as, if the event was certain to occur, the estate would not qualify as a fee simple, which is an estate that has the potential to last for ever.

For example, Gerry disposed of land 'To Ian in fee simple until David dies'. Given that it is certain that David will die at some time in the future, Ian does not receive a determinable fee. However, the transaction 'To Ian in fee simple so long as Northern Ireland remains part of the UK' is properly constituted. If Northern Ireland unites with the Republic then Ian's fee simple ends and the estate reverts back to Gerry. Gerry therefore enjoys the possibility that at some time in the future the land will return to him, or if he dies in the meantime, to his successors. Gerry's suspended interest is known as a *possibility of reverter*.

A fee simple upon a condition, often called a *conditional fee*, can also exist. A conditional fee is a fee simple that is attached to a *condition subsequent*, which if breached, may cause the estate to end. A condition subsequent must be distinguished from a *condition precedent*. In brief, a condition precedent is a condition that must be satisfied first before the estate or interest becomes vested in the grantee. For example, Gerry disposes of land 'To Ian and his heirs if Ian reaches the age of 18.' In this, Ian must become 18 before he obtains the fee simple; this is a condition precedent.

A condition subsequent is a condition that may result in the forfeiture of an estate already vested in the grantee. For example, Gerry disposes of land 'To Ian and his heirs provided Ian remains a solicitor'. This is a condition subsequent; Ian receives a fee simple but may lose it if he ceases to be a solicitor and Gerry may then have what is termed a *right of re-entry*.

The final issue that arises as regards modified fee simples is how to distinguish between a determinable fee and a conditional fee. In the case of a *determinable fee* the words describing the determining event are deemed to be part of the words of limitation — they have the potential to delimit the duration of the estate. It follows that in the case of a determinable fee, when the specified event occurs, the fee simple comes to its natural end (*determination*) according to the words of limitation and the possibility of reverter takes effect automatically to confer the fee simple absolute on the grantor or his successor.

In the case of a *conditional fee*, the terms of the condition are not deemed part of the words of limitation and are seen as independent words of condition. It follows that in the case of a conditional fee, if the condition fails or is breached, the estate does not automatically end as, until the grantor exercises his right of re-entry, no forfeiture is said to occur and the grantee continues to hold his estate.

Porter, M.R., in *Re King's Trust* (1892) 29 L R Ir 401, described the complexity of the distinction as little short of disgraceful and virtually unintelligible. In practice, the courts have developed some shorthand methods to assist in the distinction. It seems that words and phrases such as 'while', 'during', 'until' and 'so long as' are treated as words of limitation creating a determinable fee, while phrases such as 'provided that', 'on condition that' and 'but if' are usually taken as words of condition indicative of a conditional fee.

Fee tails

The fee tail was originally designed to keep a family name associated with the prestige, power and wealth of land. It was given statutory recognition as early as the Statute de Donis Conditionalibus in 1285. The fee tail is also called the *estate tail* or *entail*, with the holder of such an estate being deemed a *tenant in tail*. The fee tail is similar to the fee simple in that it is an estate of inheritance, though it is more limited than the fee simple in that it is restricted to direct descendants of the tenant in tail.

Fee tails inter vivos

At common law an inter vivos conveyance of a fee tail is indicated by the phrase 'To A and the heirs of his body'. The words 'To A' are words of purchase and the words 'the heirs of the body' are the appropriate words of limitation.

A fee tail can be further limited into a *fee tail special*. For example, a fee tail limited to male descendants only can be created in the fashion 'To A and the heirs male of his body'. In the scenario 'To A and the heirs male of his body begotten by Teresa', A obtains a fee tail male under which the line of male descendants must originate with a child born of the union between him and Teresa.

As an alternative, Section 51 of the Conveyancing Act 1881 has stated that the phrase 'in tail' for a fee tail general and 'in tail male'/'in tail female' for a fee tail special, can be used.

Fee tails by will

Prior to the enactment of the Succession Act 1965, the words of limitation required in a conveyance of a fee tail inter vivos did not have to be used in order to create a fee tail by will. In accordance with the courts' more liberal approach to the interpretation of wills, and so long as the testator demonstrated an intention to grant the estate, the absence of the appropriate words of limitation was irrelevant. Thus, precedent can be found upholding the creation of a fee tail where the testator has used the phrase 'To A and his issue', 'To A and his descendants' or, confusingly, 'To A and his heirs'; see further *Re Waugh* [1903] 1 Ch 744.

Section 95(1) of the Succession Act 1965 prohibited this flexible, intention-based approach. Under Section 95(1) an estate tail may be created by will only by the use of the same words of limitation permitted in respect of a conveyance inter vivos.

Barring the entail

The immediate possessor of land under an entail has a restricted estate. The succession to the land is out of his hands, thus, not alone is the land kept from the market place, but the possessor of the land has little incentive to manage the land in question. To escape these fetters a practice called *barring the entail* developed.

This practice was given statutory recognition by the Fines and Recoveries (Ireland) Act 1834. In brief, where the tenant in tail wished to have the freedom to deal with the land, he could now execute a *disentailing assurance*, which in effect states that the fee tail is enlarged into a fee simple. In validation, this deed of conveyance would then be lodged in the High Court as per Section 39 of the Act.

Where the tenant in tail is in immediate possession of the land, then the disentailing procedure can occur in a straightforward manner. However, the execution of the assurance by the tenant in tail will not be sufficient where a freeholder other than the tenant in tail is in possession of the land. Under Section 32 of the 1834 Act, the freeholder in possession is the *protector of the settlement* and the protector must consent to the execution of the assurance if it is to be fully effective. If the consent of the protector is not obtained and the disentailing assurance is not properly enrolled in the High Court then the assurance will not enlarge the fee tail into an absolute fee simple but into what is known as a *base fee*, defined as a fee simple that arises when an entail has not been fully barred.

Given the incomplete nature of the base fee it is an extremely unattractive commercial asset. The 1834 Act recognised this and allowed the holder of the base fee to enlarge it into a fee simple absolute. This enlargement can occur in a number of ways. First, the base fee can be enlarged into a fee simple absolute if its holder simply executes a fresh disentailing assurance, with the consent of the protector or, alternatively, the holder of the base fee can wait for the end of the protectorship, for example, the death of the freeholder in possession; see Sections 16 and 33 of the 1834 Act. Secondly, the holder of the base fee may enlarge it by simply buying out the immediate fee simple remainder or reversion and Section 37 of the 1834 Act provides that in this purchase the base fee is enlarged into a fee simple absolute free of all claims by the issue in tail or any reversioners or remaindermen taking after them. Finally, the current holder of the base fee may enlarge it into a fee simple by acquiring title to the fee simple by way of the doctrine of adverse possession, that is, by remaining in possession of the land for 12 years after the protectorship has ended.

By permitting the relatively facile conversion of the fee tail into a fee simple, the 1834 statute acts as a disincentive to the creation of the fee tail estate. In modern terms, the fee tail is rarely encountered and it is almost obsolete. The Law Reform Commission implicitly acknowledged this in 1989. The Commission did not, however, recommend the abolition of the estate on the rather glib grounds that the estate 'wasn't doing any harm'; see further Land Law and Conveyancing Law: (1) General Proposals (LRC 30, 1989), p. 6.

Life estates

The life estate is the oldest of the freehold estates. The life estate's duration is measured by reference to the life span of the person to whom it is granted. This person is the *life tenant*; for example, 'To A for life' implies that A receives a life estate.

There is also the possibility of disposing land to a person for a duration that depends on the life of another. This is an *estate pur autre vie* and the person whose life dictates the length of the estate is the *cestui que vie*. For example, Gerry disposes land 'To Ian for the life of David'. David is the cestui and Ian's estate will end on David's death.

The rule in Shelley's case

This rule may entitle the grantee to an estate of inheritance (either a fee tail or a fee simple), even though the transaction under which the land is given omits the appropriate words of limitation and instead purports to give an estate to his heirs. The rule is often stated in the following manner:

> It is a rule of law that when an estate of freehold is given to a person, and by the same disposition an estate is limited either mediately or immediately to his heirs [fee simple] or for the heirs of his body [fee tails] the words 'heirs' or 'heirs of the body' are words of limitation and not words of purchase.

In many ways the rule in Shelley's case operates on a merger principle in which the appropriate words of limitation are chosen to uphold an estate of inheritance. For example, at first look at the disposition 'To A for life remainder to A's heirs', it seems that A receives a life estate with the remainder going to A's heirs. Given that the remainder conveyance does not have any words of limitation appropriate to the creation of an estate of inheritance, it appears that A's heirs merely receive joint life estates.

Applying the rule in Shelley's case, both parts of the arrangement are in effect merged so that the disposition reads 'To A and his heirs', which implies that A receives a fee simple in possession.

Leasehold estates

The major classifications of leasehold estates will be dealt with in Chapter 11. The origin of the lease can be traced to the statute Quia Emptores in 1290. This provision attempted to prohibit subinfeudation and as a result the traditional pyramid of feudal interests in land began to contract. Landowners attempted to avoid this ban on subinfeudation by utilising the mechanism of the lease. A lease simply allows a person (lessee or tenant) to hold land of another (lessor or landlord) on the payment of rent. This arrangement did not infringe Quia Emptores because it did not involve the grant of a freehold estate. As a result of the demise of feudal tenure in the seventeenth century leasehold estates increased in popularity though initially the common law viewed them in contractual terms only.

Hybrid estates

One of the peculiarities of Irish land law is the number of estates which have both freehold and leasehold characteristics. Two of these hybrid estates are noteworthy, namely 'leases for lives' and 'fee farm grants'.

Leases for lives

By the nineteenth century, nearly one-seventh of land in Ireland was held under leases granted for the duration of one or more lives. The popularity of this arrangement, which combined freehold and leasehold characteristics, had two main reasons. First, as in any leasehold relationship, the lessee (tenant) paid rent to the lessor (landlord) and was also obliged to comply with various covenants and conditions contained in the lease, for example, repair and maintain covenants. Second, as the duration of the estate was based on the life (or lives) of another (or others), it was deemed a freehold estate, thereby entitling the holder to a vote in parliamentary elections, which the landlord could in turn expect to be used to his benefit or the benefit of his nominees.

Two principal categories of leases for lives were recognised. First, there was the *lease for lives renewable for ever*, which was essentially an estate pur autre vie and usually granted for the lives of three persons, for example, 'To Ian for the life of Jack, Don and Paul'. This standard form of lease also contained a covenant for perpetual renewal of these lives on payment to the landlord of a specified fine on each renewal: when one of the cestuis que vie died, the life of another person could be added on payment to the landlord of the renewal fine.

The lives chosen as cestuis que vie were usually persons known to the lessee, who was obliged to inform the landlord, when appropriate, of the need for a new cestui que vie. If this estate ended due to the failure of the lessee to, in effect, update the cestuis que vie, equity might permit the revival of the lease on payment of all outstanding rent and renewal fines to the landlord, if the circumstances of the case and conscionable behaviour of the lessee so demanded. Section 1 of the Tenantry Act (Ireland) 1779 reiterated this equitable doctrine in statutory form. The legislation also provided that the lessee was not entitled to relief where renewal fines had been demanded but had not been paid within a reasonable time frame. Similarly, where the lessee deliberately and fraudulently — in order to avoid the payment of a fine — failed to disclose the death of a cestui que vie, no relief would be granted to that lessee. Finally, under Section 37 of the Renewable Leasehold Conversion Act 1849, leases for lives renewable for ever can no longer be granted and if one attempts to do so a fee farm grant (see below) will automatically vest in the grantee.

However, leases for lives combined with a term of years can still be created today, though they do not have the potential to last for ever. In effect what we have here is an estate pur autre vie followed, on the death of the last surviving cestui que vie, by a term of years, for example, 'To Ian for the life of Jack, Don and Paul, remainder on lease for 35 years'. On the death of the last survivor of Jack, Don or Paul, the estate runs for the duration of a 35-year lease.

Fee farm grants

On the other hand, a fee farm grant exists where the holder of a fee simple is under a perpetual obligation to pay rent to the grantor of the estate. During the plantation of Ireland, and in particular during the seventeenth century, this type of estate was quite popular and effective. The resettled land was given in fee simple to the planters in return for regular money payments known originally as *quit rents*.

A more modern recognition of the fee farm grant can be found in Section 3 of the Landlord and Tenant (Amendment) Act 1860 (Deasy's Act). One of the reforms sought by Irish farmers in the latter part of the nineteenth century was the reform of the fee farm grant concept. Under the Redemption of Rent (Ireland) Act 1891, Irish tenants could redeem fee farm grants as created under Deasy's Act. In other words they could buy out the interest, as supported by loans provided, at low interest, under the Act. It is now the case that fee farm grants of any type or creation can be redeemed, and the fee simple bought absolutely, under the Landlord and Tenant (Ground Rents) (No. 2) Act 1978.

Conclusion

Of all the estates it is without question that the fee simple is the most valuable and desirable as it is the nearest the common law gets to a concept of absolute ownership of land. It has been demonstrated that the popularity and practicality of creating a fee tail has been limited by the Fines and Recoveries (Ireland) Act 1834. The life estate is of little commercial utility given the precarious nature of its duration. Leasehold estates have developed in importance to the extent that landlord and tenant law is a practically autonomous area of land law, while the hybrid estates have undergone significant statutory amendment.

Finally, any disposition of land may contain a combination of these estates in a manner that creates future interests in land. The common law has fought a long and arduous battle to regulate future interests on the grounds that they may overly restrict dealings in and the availability of land. This 'battle' will be reviewed in the next chapter.

Further reading

Coughlan, P., *Property Law*, 2nd edn. Dublin: Gill & MacMillan, 1998, Chapters 3 and 6.

Lyall, A., *Land Law in Ireland*, 2nd edn. Dublin: Round Hall Sweet & Maxwell, 2000, Chapters 6–9.

Wylie, J., *Irish Land Law*, 3rd edn. Dublin: Butterworths, 1997, Chapter 4.

Self-test

1. Discuss the nature and creation of the varieties of fee simple.

2. Outline the impact that the Fines and Recoveries (Ireland) Act 1834 had on the freehold estate known as the fee tail.

3. Why is the life estate described as being of dubious commercial value?

4
FUTURE INTERESTS

Future interests are without doubt a complex and difficult area of the law but a relatively simple definition is:

> any interests in land with respect to which the enjoyment of that land is postponed to some time in the future, if that enjoyment is ever going to occur at all.

In general, an interest in land may be:

- vested in possession
- vested in interest
- contingent.

Where a person has an interest *vested in possession*, they have an immediate right of possession. Interests that are vested in interest or contingent are known as future interests – the interest is not immediate but is delayed or postponed into the future (in futurity). Specifically, if an estate is *vested in interest*, it means that, even though the person entitled is definitively identified and even though no conditions are attached to that person's interest, some other person has the right of prior possession. A *contingent* future interest is more speculative in the sense that the name of the person to whom it is to be given cannot as of yet be identified and in any event their interest may depend on the materialisation of other events, that is, it may be conditional.

For example, where land is granted 'To Ian for life, remainder to Gerry in fee simple', Ian has a life estate vested in possession while Gerry's remainder is vested in interest. If the conveyance read 'To Ian for life, remainder to Gerry in fee simple, if he qualifies as a solicitor', then Ian has a life estate vested in possession but Gerry's remainder is contingent on him becoming a solicitor: he *must* satisfy the condition. It follows that the grant may fail because Gerry may never become a solicitor.

Clearly, it is preferable to have an estate which vests in interest as it is of more immediate and definitive value than that which is contingent. In fact, a contingent interest was seen as merely giving rise to the possibility of entitlement to the property, as the condition must first be satisfied. As a result, the common law traditionally held that contingent interests were incapable of transfer, that is, they were inalienable. However, it is now the case that contingent interests can be disposed of inter vivos by deed (Section 6 of the Real Property Act 1845) and by will (Section 76 of the Succession Act 1965).

Reversions and remainders

Future interests most frequently encountered are reversions and remainders.

Reversions

A reversion arises automatically whenever a person with a freehold estate grants to another a freehold estate that is smaller than his own. The use of the word automatically indicates that reversions do not have to be expressly created as they arise by operation of law. It follows that reversions are always vested in interest: the person entitled (the original grantor) is definitively identified, no conditions are attached to that person's interest but some other person has the right of prior possession.

In short, a reversion is that which is left over after the expiry of a lesser estate carved out of a larger estate. The lesser estate is known as the *particular estate* as it consists of only part of the larger estate. For example, Ian, the owner of a fee simple estate, grants land 'To Gerry for life'. Ian's fee simple in possession is not disposed of in its entirety and it becomes a fee simple in reversion subject to Gerry's particular life estate. Therefore, while Gerry is alive, Ian has a future interest in reversion and on Gerry's death; Ian's fee simple reverts back to his possession. Thus, a reversion may be defined as that part of a grantor's estate in property which is not disposed of by a grant.

Remainders

A reversion is a vested right to which only a grantor is entitled and there can only be one reversion in a conveyance. This is to be contrasted with a remainder, as a remainder arises when an estate in possession is granted to a person and, instead of the original grantor merely leaving the property to revert back to him on the determination of that estate, the grantor goes on in the same disposition to grant some or all of the residue of his estate to other persons. In theory, any number of remainders can be created in a single disposition but the more remote the remainder, the more likely it is to fall foul of common law remainder rules.

For example, here is a simple disposition combining both a reversion and a remainder. Ian, the owner of a fee simple estate, grants land to David for life, remainder to Gerry in fee tail. In this case, David has a life estate in possession, Gerry has a fee tail in remainder and Ian has a fee simple in reversion. On the completion of David's and Gerry's estates, the land will revert back to Ian, or his successors in title, as a fee simple in possession.

Remainders, unlike reversions, may be either vested or contingent. In a contingent remainder the grantee would not be entitled to the remainder estate until the condition was fulfilled. Thus, contingent remainders bring an element of doubt to the transaction as it is difficult, even speculative, to attempt to assess who may be entitled to the contingent interest. For this reason, the common law initially refused to recognise contingent remainders, though, eventually, the common law compromised and attempted to regulate contingent interests by use of so-called *common law remainder rules*. The principle underlying these rules was to ensure that seisin of the land (meaning that a person is entitled to freehold possession) would not be broken. The common law would not tolerate abeyance — gaps — in seisin. In other words at all times it is necessary that when an estate comes to an end there should clearly be someone entitled to the next estate so that there is an unbroken line of persons with seisin in the land.

Common law remainder rules

There is a danger with both vested and contingent remainders that, as a result of their operation, a gap in seisin could occur. The common law would not tolerate this and it regulates the validity of remainders by use of the following four rules:

1. A prior freehold estate must support a remainder.

2. A remainder must vest immediately on the determination of a prior freehold estate.

3. A remainder must not cut short a prior freehold estate.

4. There can be no remainder after a fee simple.

It must be noted that legal remainders are now a rarity. In fact, equity permits the creation of future interests by way of trust and these do not have to comply with the legal remainder rules. Remainder rules do not apply to gifts arising under the Statute of Uses or gifts by way of will.

1. *A prior freehold estate must support a remainder*. According to this rule, a grantor cannot create a future interest in land without first creating a prior particular estate. In other words, someone has to have an

immediate right to seisin. For example, Ian grants land 'To Gerry in fee simple when he reaches the age of 25'. If Gerry is under 25 at the time of the conveyance, it is void from the outset because a gap in the seisin would result. However, if Ian had supported the grant to Gerry with a prior freehold estate, Gerry's contingent interest may be a valid remainder. For example, Ian grants land 'To David for life, remainder to Gerry in fee simple when he reaches 25'. Here the gap in seisin is plugged by David's life estate, as it is possible that by the time this life estate ends, Gerry will have reached 25.

Given the definition of seisin — freehold possession of land — any gap in the seisin must be plugged by a freehold estate. For example, David grants land 'To Ian for 10 years, remainder to Gerry in fee simple when he reaches the age of 25'. Here a valid prior leasehold estate is created but as leasehold estates were not considered to carry seisin, a 10-year gap in seisin is said to arise and Gerry's contingent remainder is void.

2. *A remainder must vest immediately on the determination of a prior freehold estate.* Just as Rule 1 states that there should be no gap in the seisin at the time of the initial grant, similarly, Rule 2 states that in the grant there should be no gap in seisin between the ending of one estate and the beginning of another. Where it is apparent from the grant that a gap in seisin will occur between the ending of the particular estate and the commencement of the remainder, the remainder will be void. For example, where land is granted 'To Ian for life, remainder to Gerry in fee simple one day after Ian's life', it is a foregone conclusion that Gerry's fee simple in remainder is void because it is to take effect after the lapse of one day during which no one has seisin.

3. *A remainder must not cut short a prior freehold estate.* As in the above rules, the reminder must vest or occur seamlessly out of the prior particular freehold estate. However, this common law remainder rule makes it clear that in doing so it must not cut short the prior freehold estate. In effect, a remainder, which purports to take effect by terminating someone else's estate prematurely, will not be a recognised remainder at law. For example, where land is granted 'To Ian for life, but, if he marries Kay, to David in fee simple', David's remainder in fee simple is void as the condition on which it depends may prematurely cut short Ian's life estate. It would be better if the grant read 'To Ian for life or until he marries Kay, remainder to David in fee simple'. Here David's remainder is valid, as the contingency does not invalidate Ian's particular estate.

4. *There can be no remainder after a fee simple.* The final rule is straightforward. The fee simple is the largest estate known to land law, therefore an effective remainder cannot be created after a fee simple because by making a grant in fee simple the grantor has exhausted the entirety of his estate — there is nothing left in remainder. For example, where David grants land 'To Ian in fee simple, remainder to Gerry in fee simple', then by virtue of this rule Gerry's fee simple is void.

Restrictions on the creation of future interests

It is a fundamental principle of land law that land — despite the understandable desire of the paper owner to determine its future — should, as far as practicable, be freely alienable as an unfettered market commodity. Future interests, and in particular remainders, seem to violate this principle in that there is the possibility that such dispositions may tie up or fetter the land for too long into the future. As noted above, there is a danger with future interests that not only could a gap in seisin appear but that the seisin in the land itself could become diluted or, in legal terms, *remote*. In line with this policy and in order to rein in or regulate future interests, the common law designed a number of rules called rules against remoteness. The most important of these rules is the (modern) rule against perpetuities though the residual authority of the so-called rule in *Whitby* v *Mitchell* also requires mention.

The rule in Whitby v Mitchell

The fee tail, as a limited freehold estate, was created to ensure that land remained in the family name. It is restricted to the direct descendants of the tenant in tail. However, as noted in Chapter 3, a process called *barring the entail* developed whereby the tenant in tail could, under circumstances regulated by the Fines and Recoveries (Ireland) Act 1834, enlarge the fee tail into a fee simple and consequently be free to alienate the property as he saw fit. As a result, the very objective of the fee tail could be circumvented.

Not surprisingly, attempts were made to convey land in such a way as to achieve the same effect as a fee tail but without leaving anyone in a position to obtain a fee simple through barring the entail. One such mechanism was known as *perpetual freehold*, which essentially was a series of life estates. A typical example went as follows: 'To Ian for life, remainder to Ian's eldest son for life, remainder to his son's children for life, and so on ...'. The important point with this arrangement was that the land remained in the family name but at no stage would anyone have an entail that could be barred.

In brief, the rule in *Whitby* v *Mitchell* (1890) 44 Ch D 85 was devised to prevent the creation of a potentially never-ending line of life estates stretching into the future. The rule is generally summarised as follows:

> Where an interest in land is conveyed or given to an unborn person, any remainder over to that unborn person's issue and any subsequent limitations are void.

Take, for example, a gift of land (the rule only applies to realty) 'To Ian for life, remainder to Ian's first-born son for life, remainder to Ian's son's first-born son for life'. If, at the date of the gift, Ian has no son, then the remainder to Ian's son's first-born son is void as a violation of the rule in *Whitby* v *Mitchell*.

In modern terms, the rule in *Whitby* v *Mitchell* has been seen as a rather harsh rule, particularly as regards gifts by will where a strict application of the rule may be used to defeat the genuine intention of the testator. Indeed, with regard to gifts by will the rule in *Whitby* v *Mitchell* may itself be circumvented by the courts. In interpreting the terms of a will that would otherwise fall foul of the rule, the courts may interpret the clause so as to achieve something approaching the result desired by the testator. This principle of endeavouring to uphold the testator's true intention is known as the *cy-près* doctrine.

If the disposition outlined above appeared in a will, it seems that the *cy-près* doctrine would allow the disposition to be construed as conferring a fee tail — instead of a life estate — on the unborn person and so, in our example, Ian's son would be deemed a tenant in tail. Although an entail can be barred, this application of the *cy-près* doctrine leaves the issue with the possibility of taking the land under the entail, and the testator's primary intention — that the land remain with the family for succeeding generations — is, as far as possible, accommodated.

It must be noted that in accordance with Section 95(1) of the Succession Act 1965 an estate tail may be created by will only by the use of the same words of limitation permitted in respect of a conveyance inter vivos, that is, by use of the strict technical language; thus, in the above context, the *cy-près* doctrine has probably been eliminated in this jurisdiction.

The rule against perpetuities

It is suggested that the modern rule against perpetuities is the mother of all the rules against remoteness. It basically states that a future interest is void from the outset if it is possible that it will not vest within the perpetuity period. The perpetuity period is a life (or lives) in being plus a period of 21 years.

The rule applies to all future interests, though it must be noted that so long as the interest vests within the perpetuity period, it is irrelevant that it might not vest in possession for a very long time. The interpretation of the rule is very strict in that the mere possibility that the interest might vest outside the perpetuity period is enough to render it void. The common law does not permit a 'wait and see' policy as to whether the eventual vesting will occur within the period. In fact in applying the rule, only circumstances pertaining at the time the disposition takes effect can be taken into account, what happens subsequently is irrelevant, even if it transpires that the vesting can, and probably will, occur within the perpetuity period.

Possibilities

As stated above, the mere possibility that at the time of the disposition the period may be exceeded is sufficient to invalidate it; see further *Re Wood* [1894] 3 Ch 381. In the instant case, the testator directed that certain gravel pits were to be operated until they were exhausted. The land was then to be sold and the proceeds distributed amongst any issue of the testator who were alive at this time. At the time of the testator's death, no one was quite sure when the pit would be fully exhausted. An estimate of four years was forwarded — it in fact took six — still well within the perpetuity period. However, it was held that the gift infringed the rule against perpetuities because at the time of the testator's death it was not certain that exhaustion would occur within the perpetuity period.

Thus, the slightest possibility of vesting occurring outside the period is fatal. However, in the past, English courts have taken this to ridiculous levels; see further *Re Dawson* (1888) 39 Ch D 155, where Chitty, J., held that the disposition was void because of the possibility of the main beneficiary in question having another child, which under the terms of the disposition would violate the perpetuity period. The fact that the woman in question was over 60 years of age and in medical terms beyond the age of childbearing was not taken into account by the court. The situation where, for the purposes of the rule against perpetuities, a woman is deemed capable of bearing children at any age is known as the *fertile octogenarian anomaly*; see further *Ward v Van der Loeff* [1924] AC 653.

Gavan Duffy, J., ridiculed the concept of a fertile octogenarian in *Exham v Beamish* [1939] IR 366. According to Gavan Duffy, J., the concept belied common sense and was probably repugnant to the Irish Constitution. Nevertheless, it may be interesting to note the effect modern fertility treatments may, in the future, have on the rule against perpetuities.

At the other end of the scale is *Re Gaite's Will Trusts* [1949] 1 All ER 459. In that case, the perpetuity period could have been breached only if a toddler of less than five years of age gave birth. This possibility is known as the _precocious toddler anomaly_. It must be noted that the judge in that case would have declared the gift void only that the toddler's child would have been illegitimate, and not within the terms of the gift as English law then stood.

Lives in being

Central to the operation of the rule against perpetuities is the perpetuity period. There are two elements to the perpetuity period (the lives in being plus 21 years):

- The life in being must be human; see further Meredith, J., in _Re Kelly_ [1932] IR 255, p. 260.
- The 'human' must, as a life in being, be alive when the disposition takes effect, and the duration of the life must govern the vesting of the future interest.

Although the lives in being are usually those of beneficiaries, there is no requirement that there should be such a connection. Therefore, it is possible to select a number of complete strangers whose lives can be used to calculate the perpetuity period and because the 21-year term does not begin to run until the death of the last surviving life in being, the selection of a large number of lives enables one to take advantage of long life spans and provide for the postponement of vesting for as long as possible without breaching the rule.

Selections of a large number of complete strangers whose lives can be used to calculate the perpetuity period, are often called _saving clauses_. Traditionally, one of the most popular manifestations of a saving clause was the _royal lives_ clause. This clause incorporates the life spans of descendants of a particular monarch alive at the date of the disposition; see further _Re Villar_ [1929] 1 Ch 243, where it was provided that an interest was not to vest until 20 years after the death of the last survivor of all lineal descendants of Queen Victoria who were alive at the time of the testator's death. When the testator died there were approximately 120 qualified lives in being.

In _Villar_ it was held that the disposition was valid because it was possible to monitor the lives in being and determine when the last one died with a degree of certainty; see further _Re Leverhulme_ (No. 2) [1943] 2 All ER 274. However, any lack of certainty will render the disposition void. For example, in _Re Moore_ [1901] 1 Ch 936, a gift in a will postponed vesting until 21 years after the death of the last survivor of all persons living at the time of the testatrix's death. This was held to be void for uncertainty as it was clearly impossible to identify the last surviving member of the earth's population who had been in existence at that relevant time; see further *O'Byrne* v *Davoren* [1994] 3 IR 373. In that case a woman left in her will a bequest directing that certain monies were to be left to the children, grandchildren and direct descendants of named persons. Mr Justice Murphy declared the bequest void on the grounds that the definition of 'descendants' was too broad, indefinite and without limit, thereby clearly breaching the rule against perpetuities.

The perpetuity period of a life or lives in being together with 21 years can be extended by up to nine months to take into account the time between the conception of a child and its birth — the gestation period. A child that had been conceived but has not yet been born is referred to in this context as a child *en ventre sa mère*.

The reform and clarification of the rule against perpetuities

It is suggested that the majority of gifts that fall foul of the rule against perpetuities do so due to incompetent or clumsy draftsmanship. Their failure cannot be attributed to any sinister or evasive motivations. Moreover, it is submitted that a strict application of the rule against perpetuities has resulted in some plainly ridiculous outcomes. It is unsurprising that a number of exceptions to the rule against perpetuities have evolved. The following are five examples of future interests that operate outside the application of the rule against perpetuities:

1. The possibility of reverter arising on the determination of a determinable fee simple; see further *AG* v *Cummins* [1906] 1 IR 406.

2. Limitations taking effect immediately upon the determination of a fee tail; see further *Nicolls* v *Sheffield* (1787) 2 Bro CC 215.

3. Rights contained in mortgages may be recognised as valid without needing to comply with the rule against perpetuities; see further *Knightsbridge Estates* v *Byrne* [1940] AC 613.

4. Rights of re-entry in the forfeiture of a lease; see further *Re Garde Browne* [1911] 1 IR 205.

5. Dispositions in favour of charities; see further *Re Worth Library* [1995] 2 IR 301.

Some of these arrangements fetter property within a period longer than the perpetuity period. Nevertheless, they are recognised as valid because, generally, these future interests are deemed to have their own internal mechanisms which render the application of the rule unnecessary.

It is clear that in the Republic of Ireland, the rule against perpetuities is in need of statutory reform. This statutory reform could simply take the form of legislation that allows beneficiaries aggrieved with the remoteness of vesting to apply to the court for an amendment of the disposition. Alternatively, statutory reform could be based on the Northern Ireland model – the Perpetuities Act (Northern Ireland) 1966. This Act considerably modifies the rule against perpetuities. Examples of these modifications include Section 3 of the Act, which introduces a flexible 'wait and see' policy. The rule can no longer render gifts void on the grounds that there is a possibility that the perpetuity period will be breached. Section 3 permits a 'wait and see' policy until such time as it is certain that the gift will occur outside the period. These 'wait and see' provisions can apply to an alternative fixed perpetuity period in that Section 1 of the Act permits the express designation of a perpetuity period of a set number of years, not exceeding 80 years. This set and certain period prevents, for example, the need to base the disposition on a saving clause such as a royal lives clause.

Furthermore, Section 2 of the Act states that males under 14 years of age and females under 12 and over 55 are now presumed incapable of child bearing, thus, eliminating the concepts of the precocious toddler and fertile octogenarian to the extent that the above presumptions may still be rebutted by evidence.

Notwithstanding the above, in 2000, the Irish Law Reform Commission issued a report: 'Land Law: Ruling Against Perpetuities' (LRC 62, 2000), which recommended the total abolition of the rule against perpetuities (and in its wake the abolition of the rule in *Whitby* v *Mitchell*). While the report acknowledged that other jurisdictions, such as Northern Ireland, merely amended the rule, the report argued that this was an overly conservative approach. The report pointed out that the experienced and alert solicitor could easily circumvent the application of the rule against perpetuities. The report argued that the rule now applies simply as a trap for the unwary or inexperienced conveyancer. Such an objective is not a reasonable basis for any rule of law. The report concluded by suggesting (and indeed drafting) a *Perpetuities Bill* under which the rule would be abolished.

Further reading

Coughlan, P., *Property Law*, 2nd edn. Dublin: Gill & MacMillan, 1998, Chapter 9.

Lyall, A., *Land Law in Ireland*, 2nd edn. Dublin: Round Hall Sweet & Maxwell, 2000, Chapter 10.

Wylie, J., *Irish Land Law*, 3rd edn. Dublin: Butterworths, 1997, Chapter 5.

Self-test

1. Central to the operation of land law is its attempt, on the one hand, to balance the understandable desire of landowners to control the future ownership and use of their property; and, on the other, the policy desire that land should, as far as is practicable, be freely alienable as an unfettered market commodity. This attitude of the law has resulted in the evolution of several rules restricting the powers of landowners to tie up land in the future.

   Briefly outline the evolution and application of the rules referred to in the above statement.

2. Apply the rule against perpetuities to the following scenario of a gift:

   To Teresa for life, then to any husband she may marry for his life, then to such of Teresa's children as shall be living at the death of the survivor of Teresa and any such husband.

Key points

The modern rule against perpetuities states that any future interest in any property is void from the outset if it may possibly breach the perpetuity period, where the perpetuity period consists of any life or lives in being plus 21 years, having regard also to any period of gestation. In the above scenario we are applying the rule to the so-called *unborn spouse trap*.

Our example may be viewed in three parts. First, Teresa obtains a vested and valid life estate. Second, on Teresa's death, any husband she may marry will also obtain a vested and valid life estate. Third, to obtain the gift the children must survive both Teresa and her husband, that is, the gift to the children is contingent upon, and will not vest until, the death of both Teresa and her husband.

It follows that Teresa and her husband are the lives in being. The perpetuity period states that the gift need only vest in the children within 21 years after the death of the last surviving life in being. At first instance this seems very likely to occur in our disposition. Nevertheless, the traditional and strict approach to the rule against perpetuities means that we must ask if there is any possibility — no matter how improbable — that the perpetuity period could be breached.

And there is a possibility. The possibility is that Teresa may marry a man who was unborn at the date of the gift and so cannot be a life in being. If he survives her by more than 21 years, vesting would occur outside the perpetuity period. The gift to the children is void.

Finally, note that Section 5 of the Perpetuities Act (Northern Ireland) 1966 has a saving provision for the unborn spouse trap based on an extended waiting period.

5
INCORPOREAL HEREDITAMENTS

Apart from leasehold and freehold estates, various minor interests in land have also come to be recognised. These interests are again feudal in origin and are known as incorporeal hereditaments. In brief, the key to an incorporeal hereditament is that its ownership confers certain rights over the land in question but not the right to possession of the land itself. It follows that the law of incorporeal hereditaments concerns the extent and application of the rights that the holder of this minor interest (or interests) has over someone else's land.

Using a right of way as an example, the basic characteristics of incorporeal hereditaments are that in many cases these interests are minor in nature; they may be infrequently invoked; they are generally of little inherent commercial value in themselves; they often concern neighbouring, adjoining lands; and, as these interests are recognised by the common law, they can be enforced against and by the successors in title to the parties who originally created them.

Nevertheless, while these interests are often minor and infrequent, the law of incorporeal hereditaments is traditionally a highly litigated area of Irish land law. Though the actual commercial value of such interests may be negligible, the strategic importance of an incorporeal hereditament may be vital to the full enjoyment of the land in question.

Classifications

Easements and *profits à prendre* (profits) are by far the most common type of incorporeal hereditaments. An easement is a right that a landowner has, by virtue of his ownership of land, over the land of his neighbour, for example, a right of way, or a right to light or to water. Many landowners have one or more of these rights. Easements are usually concerned with adjoining pieces of property. A *profit à prendre* is not necessarily confined to neighbouring lands but is said to exist 'in gross', that is, independently of any land owned by the holder of the profit. In essence, a profit is the right to enter another person's land in order to take something from that land that is regarded as belonging to it naturally, for example, timber, turf, minerals or fish.

This chapter will concentrate almost exclusively on easements and profits. Other categories of incorporeal hereditaments include periodic or ground rents, various land annuities and franchises. Franchises, for example, were originally exclusive rights or privileges granted by the Crown to individual subjects or local authorities, for example, the right to hold fairs and markets, the right to run ferries, the right to wrecks and treasure trove and free fishing rights; see further *R (Moore)* v *O'Hanrahan* [1927] IR 406, *Moore* v *AG* [1934] IR 44, *Little* v *Cooper* [1937] IR 1, *AG* v *Cooper* [1956] IR 1 and *ESB* v *Gormley* [1985] ILRM 494.

Easements

There are four essential features of an easement:

- *Dominant and servient tenements.* While a profit is said to exist in gross, that is not the case as regards an easement. The concept of an easement generally, but not necessarily nor always, involves the existence of two parcels of adjoining land. These two parcels of land are called the dominant and servient tenements. The dominant tenement is the land benefited by the easement and the servient tenement is the land over which the easement exists, for example, X, the owner of Blackacre has a right of way over Whiteacre, which is owned by X's neighbour Y. Thus, Blackacre is the dominant tenement and Whiteacre is the servient tenement. A discussion of dominant and servient tenements can be located in *Gaw* v *CIE* [1953] IR 232 and *Scott* v *Goulding* Properties [1973] IR 200.
- *Accommodation of the dominant tenement.* It is not enough that the easement benefits the owner of the dominant land in his personal capacity, it is said that the easement must benefit or accommodate the land — it must improve the land in terms of amenity. In other words, if the easement is interfered with, will this make the dominant property less convenient to use or enjoy? An effective example of this principle in action is the easement of the right to light. For example, a new construction or some other interference in an adjoining piece of land interferes with the amount of light previously entering a building on the dominant land. In these circumstances, and where the easement of light is proved to exist, the easement can be invoked to prevent against the diminution of light; see further *McGrath* v *Munster and Leinster Bank* [1959] IR 313.
- *Ownership or occupation by different persons.* An easement is essentially an interest held by one person over another person's land. It follows as a general rule that the dominant and servient tenements must be held under separate ownership. This general rule may be qualified in a situation where there is common ownership but different occupiers of

land; for example, it is well held that a tenant may have an easement in respect of land occupied by his immediate landlord or another tenant of the same landlord; see further *Hanna* v *Pollock* [1900] 2 IR 664, *Flynn* v *Harte* [1913] 2 IR 322 and *Tallon* v *Ennis* [1937] IR 549.

* *Subject matter of a grant*. The fourth essential feature of an easement is that the alleged easement should be capable of precise definition so that it can, if necessary, be described accurately as the subject matter of a grant. It is for this reason that many alleged easements of light fail as there is some confusion between the right to light and the mere right to a view which is not a recognised easement; see further *Scott* v *Goulding* [1973] IR 200. Accordingly, if there is any doubt as regards a right it is better for the claimant to secure that right in the form of a restrictive covenant.

Typical easements

The most typical easements are the right of way, right to light, right of water and right of support.

Right of way

A right of way may be *general* in the sense that it can be used at any time, or *limited*, in the sense that some restriction binds the dominant owner or user; see further *Tubridy* v *Walsh* (1901) 35 ILT 321 where there was an obligation on the dominant user to close the gates. One of the more contentious issues as regards rights of way is the maintenance of the right of way. As a general rule, the user must maintain the right of way although this may be subject to a separate agreement between the parties; see further *Gaw* v *CIE* [1953] IR 232.

Right to light

A right to light can be acquired for a building, a side of a building, or even in some cases an individual window. It is now firmly established that the right to light to which a dominant owner is entitled must be limited. The amount of light which the dominant owner can lay claim to is the objective standard of that which the reasonable user would need to facilitate the proper enjoyment of his property; see further *Sermon* v *Bradford Corporation* [1922] 2 Ch 737, *McGrath* v *Munster and Leinster Bank Ltd* [1959] IR 313 and *Scott* v *Goulding* [1973] IR 200.

Right to water

An example of this easement would include the right to a flow or discharge of water from or to the servient land, be it a natural watercourse or via artificial means; see further *Hanna* v *Pollock* [1900] 2 IR 664. The right to water cattle in a stream could also be included in this category; see further *Re Harding's Estate* (1874) IR 8 Eq 620.

The dominant owner may be entitled to enter the servient owner's land to remove any obstruction to the flow of the water.

Right of support

Mutual rights of support invariably exist where buildings keep each other standing, as in terraced housing. In practice, this means that the servient owner must take reasonable care to maintain his premises so that the support given by his premises will not adversely affect the dominant owner. In certain circumstances, the dominant owner may protect himself by entering onto the neighbouring property to maintain its repair; see further *Jones* v *Pritchard* [1908] 1 Ch 630 and *Bond* v *Nottingham Corporation* [1940] Ch 429.

A recent Irish case on the right of support is *Todd* v *Cinelli and others*, 12 April 1999, ITLR. Two semi-detached houses had been built as one. One of them was demolished and in the circumstances this was held to be a breach of the easement of support entitling the neighbouring landowners to damages for the change of appearance of their house.

Future and negative easements

It must be noted that the above list of typical easements is not exhaustive and must, like all law, expand with the changes of modern life. It is suggested that a new category of easements may well arise regarding the laying of pipes and cables, which necessarily traverse neighbouring properties. There is an overlap here with the concept of a *wayleave*, which can be defined as the right over another's land to facilitate the supply of utility services such as water, electricity or gas.

It must also be noted that the courts are wary of developing new easements particularly where the easement that is claimed by the dominant owner is of a *negative* variety, that is, preventing the servient owner from doing something on his own land which he would otherwise be entitled to do. This is to be contrasted with a *positive* easement, which normally allows the dominant owner to do something on the servient owner's land; see further *Treacy* v *Dublin Corporation* [1993] 1 IR 305 where it was claimed by the dominant occupier that if the servient occupier knocked down the building in question, the dominant occupier's right to shade and shelter would be affected and his property would be exposed to the elements.

Profits à prendre

Profits are the right to take something from another person's land, the general rule being that the 'something' must be part of the land itself, for example, minerals, turf, wild game or fish. However, water, which also occurs naturally on the land, cannot be owned and cannot be the subject of a profit — though it can, as we have demonstrated, be the subject of an easement.

Similar to an easement, a profit may be created *appurtenant* (annexed) to some parcel of land, that is, to benefit that land. In such a case the profit must comply with the four essential features necessary for an easement and generally a profit appurtenant must be confined to the needs of the dominant tenement; see further *Cronin v Connor* [1913] 2 IR 119. A *profit appurtenant* is a profit annexed to land by an act of the parties in question, whereas a profit annexed to the land by operation of the law is known as a *profit appendant*. The most common example of a *profit appendant* was the ancient feudal right of common pasturage whereby the freehold grantee of arable manor land had, as an appendant to that land, a right to pasture certain animals at certain periods of the year on manor wasteland. Such a grant of freehold land within a manor was deemed subinfeudation and therefore no new *profits appendants* could be created after Quia Emptoires, 1290 (see Chapter 3).

Finally, as has already been mentioned, unlike an easement, a profit can also be enjoyed independently of any dominant tenement – it can exist in gross. It follows that profits *in gross* clearly do not need to comply with all four requirements for an easement.

The following are the most common *profits à prendre*.

Pasturage

This is the right to graze animals on someone else's land. In the past such rights were held in common with other farmers in the locality. Several rights in common survived in the West of Ireland until fairly recently; see further *Re Commonage at Glennamaddoo* [1992] 1 IR 297.

Turbary

This is the right to go onto another person's land and to cut and take away turf. This profit is in many ways subject to customary law, with the degree of freedom given to the grantee varying from bog to bog. For example, in some bogs the grantee is limited to a certain patch, in others there is a more general right. In a general sense, the Republic of Ireland has seen the acquisition of much of the State's prime peat areas by the semi-state company, Bórd na Móna.

Mines and quarries

Mining and quarrying rights, whether relating to existing mines or quarries or for the opening of new mines or quarries, are another common form of *profit à prendre*. However, many minerals are extremely valuable and the pattern of recent decades has been for the State to exercise increasing control over minerals and their exploitation; see further Article 10 of the Irish Constitution, *Comyn v AG* [1950] IR 142 and *Tara Prospecting v Minister for Energy* [1993] ILRM 771.

Fisheries

Large stretches of the Irish inland waterway network are subject to private fishing rights, which the various Fishery Acts have attempted to regulate. In *Gannon v Walsh* [1998] 3 IR 245, the plaintiffs had a fisheries profit on part of the river Moy. The plaintiffs sold permits which allowed professional anglers to fish on this part of the river. The owners of the land bordering the river (known as the *riparian owners*) became upset at the number of people who were taking shortcuts through their lands to fish on the river.

The defendants blocked the only pathway to the river and the plaintiffs sought an injunction to prevent this action. Keane, J., (as he then was) argued that the grant of fishing rights as an incorporeal hereditament implies a right of access to the banks of the river or lake over which the rights are exercisable. However, the right of access must be exercised in a manner which causes the least possible detriment to the riparian owner, that is, a balance must be struck. In a practical sense, the balance struck in this instance was that the anglers could not drive down the pathway to the riverbank but should walk.

Sporting rights

In addition to fishing rights, it is common to have grants or reservations made of other sporting rights such as the hunting and shooting of wild animals and fowl.

Similar concepts

There are several other concepts recognised by land law that share many of the characteristics of easements and profits, but which must be distinguished from them.

Natural rights

It can be quite difficult at times to distinguish between a natural right and an easement. In theory, the difference is that an easement must be acquired, whereas a natural right exists automatically in respect of land. In practice, this means that a plaintiff's task in court is much easier if he can base his claim on a natural right under the law of torts instead of having to prove the acquired existence of an easement under land law.

One example that demonstrates the difference between the two concepts is that of the right to support. The natural right to support is confined to land in its natural state and this natural right will be breached if the actions of the other party literally undermine or erode the soil support of the dominant tenement; see further *Latimer* v *Official Co-op Society* (1885) 16 LR Ir 305. No natural right of support exists in respect of buildings on the land; such a right in respect of buildings must be acquired as an easement; see further *Green* v *Belfast Tramways* (1887) 20 LR Ir 35 and *Todd* v *Cinelli and others*, 12 April 1999, ITLR.

Public rights

Certain public rights are very similar to rights also recognised as easements or profits; for example, there can be a public right of way over land. The essential difference between such a right and an easement is that the public right of way can be invoked by any member of the public, regardless of their ownership of dominant land. Traditionally, at common law, a public right of way could be created by what was known as *dedication and acceptance* — the owner of the land dedicates the way to the public, and the public then accepts that dedication. The owner usually makes the dedication informally and the public acceptance is inferred through long usage; see further *Smeltzer* v *Fingal Co.* [1998] 1 IR 279.

Local customary rights

Similar to public rights, local customary rights differ from easements in that they are not necessarily annexed to any dominant land. However, local customary rights differ from public rights in that they are confined to members of a local community. Local customary rights are recognised at common law provided they satisfy four basic requirements, being:

- ancient
- certain
- reasonable
- continuous.

Ancient is taken to mean dating back to or before the beginning of legal memory, which according to the Statute of Westminster I 1275 is 1189. Nevertheless, in practice the courts are prepared to presume ancient origin provided long enjoyment of 20–40 years is shown and that no proof of an origin later than 1189 can contradict this.

An example of a local customary right in action is in the case of *Abercromby* v *Town Commissioners of Fermoy* [1900] 1 IR 302. The owner of a riverbank brought an action in declaration of title contrary to the long use of this strip of land by the Fermoy townspeople as a promenade. Holmes, L.J., held that the plaintiff was undoubtedly the owner of the land in question but his ownership was subject to the local customary right of the inhabitants to use the land for recreational purposes.

The acquisition of incorporeal hereditaments

An easement or profit can be acquired through any of the following procedures.

Statute

During the plantation era in Ireland, many of the settlers received, as part of their settlement from the Crown, various easements and profits in addition to their land; see further *Little* v *Moylett* [1929] IR 439 and *Moore* v *AG* [1934] IR 44. The profits given in these instances regularly concerned fishing rights; see further *Cooper* v *AG* [1935] IR 425 and *AG (Mahony)* v *Cooper* [1956] IR 1.

Express grants

The parties to a land transaction may create easements and profits expressly. For example, if Ian, the owner of Blackacre, sells part of that land to Gerry, Ian may as part of the sale, confer on Gerry various easements (such as a right of way) and profits (such as fishing rights) to be enjoyed by Gerry over Ian's remaining land. In other words, Gerry's plot is the dominant tenement and Ian's is the servient. This transaction is known as the express grant of an easement or profit. The usual method of expressly granting an easement or a profit is by deed, although in practice this is usually rendered superfluous as the grant of an easement or profit is usually part of a larger land transaction, which is invariably executed by deed. It is suggested that caution dictates that the appropriate words of limitation be used to make it clear for what estate that is, duration, the easement or profit is given.

Express reservations

Alternatively, when selling part of Blackacre to Gerry, Ian could reserve easements (such as the right to support) or profits (such as gaming rights) over the land sold to Gerry. Gerry is now the servient tenant. This transaction involves an express reservation of easements and profits rather than a grant. A reservation of an easement or profit will also be done by deed and must be done at the time of the conveyance to the purchaser.

Implied grants

Even if a particular conveyance does not mention the creation of easements and profits expressly, they may be created by implication on a true interpretation of the deed of conveyance. A distinction must be made here between an implied grant and an implied reservation.

The general rule as regards a grant, be it express or implicit, is that a grant is invariably construed by the courts in favour of the grantee. The underlying philosophy is that the grantor, who is in a position to dictate the terms of a transaction, should not be in a position to complain if a dispute subsequently occurs. This bias in favour of the grantee results frequently in the creation of implied easements and sometimes profits.

It seems from the case law that implied grants of easements (and sometimes profits) could arise in the following circumstances.

Easements of necessity

Where A grants part of his land to B and the only means of access to B's land is through the remainder of the plot owned by A, then out of necessity an easement of way will be created in favour of B; see further *Donnelly v Adams* [1905] 1 IR 154.

Intended easements

An intended easement is where the easement is necessary to carry out the common intention of the parties. As a result a grant will be implied in favour of the grantee; see further *Wong v Beaumont Properties* [1965] 1 QB 173.

The rule in Wheeldon v Burrows

The rule in *Wheeldon v Burrows* (1879) 12 Ch D 31 is essentially a catch-all rule governing the permissibility or otherwise of an implied grant. According to the rule, on the grant of a part of land owned by the grantor, there pass to the grantee, by way of an implied grant, easements which can be said to satisfy three tests, namely:

- They were continuous and apparent.
- They were necessary to the reasonable enjoyment of the land.
- They had been, and still were at the time of the grant, used by the grantor for the benefit of the part granted.

However, it is important to note the limitations of the application of this rule. The rule applies only to what are known as *quasi-easements*. Quasi-easements may arise in the following manner.

It is a central characteristic of an easement that the dominant and servient tenement must not be owned and occupied by the same person. A landowner cannot have an easement over his own land. However, where the owner habitually uses part of his land for the benefit and accommodation of another parcel of his land, the law may recognise a quasi-easement, to the extent that this usage has the potential to become a full easement on the sale of that part of land to another; for example, if a landowner habitually uses a defined path across part of his land to access his dwelling house. Though similar to a right of way, this practice cannot be recognised as a full easement as a landowner cannot have such a right over his own land.

However, as per *Wheeldon v Burrows*, on disposal of the parcel of land that is benefited, it may be implied into the conveyance that the quasi-easement (the quasi right of way) is converted into a full easement enforceable against the land retained by the grantor.

As noted above, the rule in *Wheeldon v Burrows* lays down that the quasi-easement must fulfil three characteristics, the first of which states that it must have been continuous and apparent. In this sense 'continuous' is taken to mean permanent as opposed to incessant use, while 'apparent' is taken to mean that if the existence of the easement cannot be seen or discovered by a reasonable inspection of the land, then it does not satisfy the test. For example, where a right of way is claimed, the presence of a worn and accessible track may be required. It is suggested that the requirements of continuity and appearance mean that the rule in *Wheeldon v Burrows* cannot apply to profits as the exercise of profits is rarely continuous and infrequently apparent.

The second requirement is that the quasi-easement must have been necessary for the reasonable enjoyment of the land granted. The emphasis here is on the word 'reasonable' and, unlike the implication of an easement of necessity, it is not necessary to establish that the land cannot be used at all without the easement.

The final requirement is simply that the rights of the quasi-easement must, prior to the grant, have had the potential to satisfy the normal requirements of an easement, for example, by accommodating the dominant–servient relationship.

Lastly, there is some debate whether or not all three requirements are necessary and a discussion of the rule's application in Ireland can be found in the aforementioned *Donnelly* v *Adams* [1905] 1 IR 154 as well as *McDonagh* v *Mullholland* [1931] IR 110.

Section 6 of the Conveyancing Act of 1881

Section 6 of the 1881 Act is a technical conveyancing device intended to shorten conveyances; it is not intended to alter or extend the categories of rights or interests recognised in land law. Section 6 operates not by implying words into a conveyance but by giving an extended meaning to general words in a manner whereby the conveyance can be construed by way of an express grant. Section 6 applies only to conveyances executed since 1881 and applies only if a contrary intention is not expressed in the conveyance, that is, Section 6 is subordinate to the terms of the conveyance.

Section 6 is important in this regard as it can operate in a manner broadly similar to the rule in *Wheeldon* v *Burrows* and may create easements out of quasi-easements; see further *International Tea Stores* v *Hobbs* [1903] 2 Ch 165 and *Wright* v *Macadam* [1949] 2 KB 744. In the latter case the right to use a shed for storing coal became an easement when a lease of certain rooms in a house was granted.

Indeed, Section 6 has a much wider application than the rule in *Wheeldon* v *Burrows* and has the capacity to be applied not only to easements but to profits as well; though it is clear that as Section 6 is a technical conveyancing provision and cannot alter substantive rights, it cannot convert into an easement or profit a right which does not initially comply with the essential requirements of an easement or profit. Moreover, Section 6 cannot — as the rule in *Wheelson* v *Burrows* can — elevate rights in a situation where an owner has used that part of his land, which he is retaining, in a manner that benefited the part to be transferred. Section 6 operates only where there has been a diversity of ownership or occupation of the dominant and servient tenements prior to the conveyance; see further *Long* v *Gowlett* [1923] 2 Ch 177. This is a considerable restriction on the section's operation, though easements of light seem to constitute an exception to this general rule; see further *Broomfield* v *Williams* [1897] 1 Ch 602.

Implied reservations

Implied reservations rarely arise as they are seen as an overly interfering and often belated attempt by the grantor to enforce a right he otherwise should have thought of. To this extent, the burden of proof required by the grantor to demonstrate an implied reservation is onerous. By far the most frequent case of easements arising by implied reservation is a reservation by way of necessity. For example, if on making a grant of part of his land, a grantor cuts himself off from part of the land he retained and becomes landlocked, there will be an implied reservation in his favour of an easement way of necessity; see further *Nickerson* v *Barraclough* [1981] Ch 426.

Presumed grants or prescription

The basis of prescription is the presumption by the courts that the right of easement or profit is of lawful origin. This presumption is proved where evidence by the claimant demonstrates that the right in question has been enjoyed by him as of right and has been continually used by him. This means that if the dominant tenant has exercised the right for a number of years, as opposed to its intermittent use, and the servient tenant has acquiesced to this, then a presumption of an easement will be recognised. If any force or secrecy was used in the acquisition of the incorporeal hereditament, then the easement or profit will not be recognised.

Three methods of prescription have come to be recognised over the centuries, namely:

- prescription at common law
- prescription under the doctrine of the lost modern grant
- prescription by statute.

Prescription at common law

At common law the courts were prepared to presume the grant of the easement or profit if the claimant could show that the incorporeal hereditament had existed and been enjoyed as of right since time immemorial — the date fixed as the limit of legal memory, 1189. Thus, a claimant in theory had to establish that he and his predecessors in title had enjoyed the easement or profit continuously since 1189. This presumption could easily be rebutted, for example, where an easement of light is claimed for a building clearly not eight centuries old. This common law doctrine was evidently unsatisfactory and the courts devised a second method of prescription known as the doctrine of lost modern grant.

Prescription under the doctrine of the lost modern grant

Under this doctrine and on evidence of 20 years' continuous usage, the courts were prepared to indulge in an alleged fiction that the easement or profit claimed was the subject of a grant executed since 1189 but that the deed of grant was now lost and so could not be produced in evidence. This legal fiction was a factual farce and an attempt was made to clarify the issue in the Prescription Act 1832, which did not apply in Ireland until 1859, with the Prescription (Ireland) Act 1858.

Prescription by statute

The Prescription Act was enacted in an effort to provide a method of prescription which would be more straightforward than the previously mentioned methods. The scheme of the Act was an attempt to consolidate and simplify the law on prescription. Its principal provisions are contained in Sections 1 and 2 which lay down two periods of continuous usage which, if fulfilled, may allow the creation of an easement or profit by prescription. The first period is 20 years for an easement and 30 years for a profit and the longer period is 40 for an easement and 60 for a profit. If the longer period can be proved the claimant will under the Act be given greater protection.

An English application of the statute can be found in *Copeland v Greenhalf* [1952] 1 Ch 488. The plaintiff owned a strip of land leading to an orchard. The plaintiff sought to restrain the defendant — a mechanic with premises across the road from the orchard — from leaving vehicles awaiting repair on the strip of land. The defendant countered that he and his father had used the strip of land (except for space to allow access to the orchard) for the storage of vehicles for 50 years; the mechanic therefore claimed a prescriptive easement under Section 2 of the Prescription Act 1832.

Upjohn, J., rejected this defence, granted the plaintiff an injunction and dismissed the defendant's counterclaim on the grounds that what he was claiming was not an easement, which is a minor interest in land, but that in practical terms the defendant was seeking 'joint user' rights of the plot to the exclusion of the owner. According to Upjohn, J., an easement is only a minor interest in the land of another, it cannot 'substantially interfere' with the rights of the owner of the land in question. In the case before him, the mechanic was, in effect, claiming exclusive possession of the strip of land; his case would have been better made out under the doctrine of adverse possession (see Chapter 8).

Extinguishment of easements and profits

There are three principal ways in which an easement or profit can be extinguished:

* by statute
* by release
* by unity of ownership and possession.

Statute

A statute may extinguish an easement or profit expressly or by implication; for example, under the Planning Acts, local authorities may have the power to compulsorily acquire land for development, thus extinguishing all easements and profits formerly attached to that land, though the owners receive compensation.

Release

The owner of an easement or profit may expressly or implicitly release it. An express release is where the owner of the incorporeal hereditament formally and by deed extinguishes his right. An implied release may arise on evidence of non-usage of the easement or profit over a long period or evidence that the easement is no longer necessary to the enjoyment of the dominant tenement; see further O'Hanlon, J., in *Carroll* v *Sheridan* [1984] ILRM 451.

Unity of ownership and possession

If the dominant and servient tenements come into the ownership and possession of the same person, then by definition the existing easements and/or profits are extinguished.

Further reading

Bland, P., *The Law of Easements and Profits à Prendre*. Dublin: Round Hall, 1997.
Coughlan, P., *Property Law*, 2nd edn. Dublin: Gill & MacMillan, 1998, Chapter 13.
Wylie, J., *Irish Land Law*, 3rd edn. Dublin: Butterworths, 1997, Chapter 6.

Self-test

Mary and Martin bought a house in a Dublin suburb in 1996. The house was semi-detached and the adjoining house, owned by Betty and John, was known as Blackacre. In June 2000, the existing rear and side extensions of Blackacre were removed, as were trees in the garden. In a local supermarket soon after this episode, Betty admitted to Martin that she and John would like to demolish the house in its entirety. Mary was slightly perturbed by this at the time but soon forgot about it.

In November 2000, Betty and John carried out further demolition works on Blackacre. The demolition was completed in a few hours, and no notice of the intention to carry out this hurried demolition was given to Mary and Martin. In fact, Mary only discovered that the works had been done when she came home from work. A shocked Mary and Martin are now concerned not only about the structural stability of their house but also the diminution in the house's value due to its extraordinary appearance in the absence of its twin. Furthermore, they have noticed that in the past week, the harsh winter frost is damaging their now exposed side wall. They seek your advice as to the legal options available to them.

Key points

The key issue here is the easement of support. First give a brief review of the concept of incorporeal hereditaments as a whole before outlining the essential characteristics of easements, such as how they are acquired and how they are extinguished. Then concentrate on specifics – the application of the easement of support. Pay particular attention to cases such as *Treacy* v *Dublin Corporation* [1993] 1 IR 305 and *Todd* v *Cinelli and others*, 12 April 1999, ITLR.

6
CO-OWNERSHIP

The common law recognises that two or more persons may simultaneously be entitled to possession of land. This is called co-ownership. For example, a husband and wife may purchase the family home in their joint names: they are co-owners of the property as a whole. Four forms of co-ownership exist:

- joint tenancy
- tenancy in common
- coparcenary
- tenancy by entireties.

Coparcenary is now extremely rare and tenancy by entireties is virtually defunct as a concept. This chapter will therefore concentrate exclusively on joint tenancies and tenancies in common. Before doing so, students must be alert to the use of the word 'tenancy' in this regard, which is used here in its broadest context and has nothing to do with leases. It merely denotes the holding of any estate or interest in land.

In both joint tenancies and tenancies in common, the co-owners share the possession of the land. Similarly, if the land is leased, the co-owners share the rental income and if the land is sold, the co-owners share the sale price. However, under a joint tenancy, when one of the co-owners dies, the survivors automatically share the whole of the land, but in a tenancy in common, the deceased co-owners' share can be passed on to another person under a will or by the rules of intestacy.

Example: joint tenancy

All co-owners of joint tenancy are alive; there is no division of ownership.

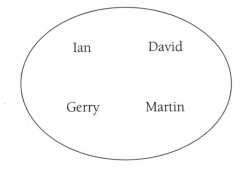

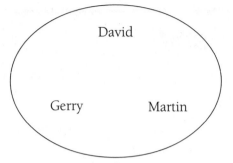

Ian dies; under a joint tenancy, the three survivors automatically share the whole of the property.

Example: tenancy in common

All co-owners of tenancy in common are alive; there is a theoretical and proportionate division of ownership.

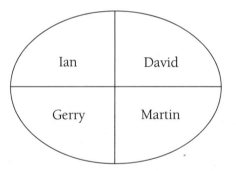

Ian dies; under a tenancy in common, Ian's successors inherit his share.

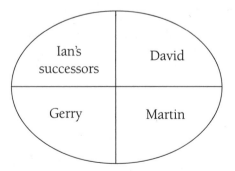

Accordingly, a joint tenancy and a tenancy in common can be distinguished by what happens on the death of one of the co-owners.

Beguile :

Foible :→

Extricate :

Sane :

Contrived :

Vociferated :

excruciation :

Doldrum :

A confusion of the heard arising from a corruption of the heart.

Nocturnes :

Impudence :

Cockscomb :

And we thereupon attested and subscribed the said will, in the presence of Marner, aforesaid, same was during, audibly, and distinctly read over to him by me and said testator appeared fully to understand the same, and was at the time of the execution thereof of sound mind, memory and understanding.

Civil Liability Act, 1961 provides

Chapter 1

Introductory

"grasp the thunderbolt"

"Law Reports on fire"

"Summing up"

"Sneer at trial by jury"

"Fine eyes of the advocate"

"Office lawyers"

glibly

8%

2% legal costs and expenses (i) date agreement (ii) date of the certificate of taxation of such costs.

Keener power of perception

entangle facts

Fallacies of Testimon

Joint tenancy

The key to a joint tenancy is that when one of the co-owners dies their interest in the property is terminated and the surviving joint tenants automatically co-own the whole of the property. This is known as the *right of survivorship* or the *jus accrescendi*. It follows that the joint tenant cannot circumvent the right of survivorship by making a will purporting to leave his share in the land to someone other than the surviving co-tenants. On death, the joint tenant's interest dies with him and cannot be disposed of by will or, indeed, under the rules of intestacy, though it can be disposed of inter vivos.

Where the joint tenants all die at the same time and it is impossible to tell whether any one survived the other for longer, for example, in a car accident, the common law holds that the heirs of the deceased joint tenants succeed to the property as joint tenants. The common law solution to the above problem of *commorientes* (simultaneous death) is preserved in Ireland by Section 5 of the Succession Act 1965.

For a joint tenancy to exist there must be four unities:

- possession
- interest
- title
- time.

Unity of possession

Each co-owner is entitled to possession of the property as a whole; see further *Lahiffe* v *Hecker*, 28 April 1994, High Court, Lynch, J. Therefore, if a joint tenant excludes or evicts a co-tenant from any part of the property, they may be liable in trespass; see further *Beaumont* v *Kinsella* (1859) 8 Ir CLR 291 and *Dennis* v *McDonald* [1982] 1 ALL ER 590. If the co-owned land is producing an income in the form of profits or rent from a third party, that income must be shared among joint tenants equally. Section 23 of the Administration of Justice (Ireland) Act 1707 permits the co-owner to sue another co-owner who obtains more than his share of any rental income or other profit from the land. This right of action is deemed a right of action of account; see further *Dawson* v *Baxter* (1887) 19 LR Ir 103.

Unity of interest

Each joint tenant must hold the same interest in the land. For example, one joint tenant cannot have a leasehold interest while the other has a freehold, similarly, one joint tenant cannot have a fee tail while the other holds a fee simple. The interest held by each joint tenant must be equal in scope and duration.

Unity of title

As joint tenants must acquire the same interest in the property, they must also acquire that interest from the same conveyance or will, that is, they must derive their title from the same document. Joint tenants can also derive title from the same act, for example, adverse possession. If members of a family remain in joint possession of property after the death of the owner, and the estate is not administered, it is held that on establishing adverse possession, these family members acquire the property as joint tenants. This scenario occurred quite frequently in rural Ireland; see further *Maher* v *Maher* [1987] ILRM 582 and *Gleeson* v *Feehan* (No. 2) [1997] ILRM 522.

Unity of time

The interest of each joint tenant should vest at the same time. For example, a father settles property on himself for life with the fee simple remainder to his children. Unity of interest is present, as all the children hold a fee simple. The requirement of unity of title is also satisfied as the children have all acquired their interest from the same conveyance. However, the requirement of unity of time will not be satisfied unless the children are all born at the date of the conveyance; if not, their rights vest at different times and a tenancy in common only is created. It is important to note that unity of time refers only to the time of vesting of an interest and not the duration of that interest.

Where the co-ownership is created by a conveyance to uses or by a disposition in a will, this final unity will not apply; see further *O'Hea* v *Slatterry* [1895] 1 IR 7.

Tenancy in common

In a tenancy in common, each tenant in common has a separate but notional share of the property as a whole. The property is not as yet physically divided to reflect the relevant shares of each tenant in common, thus, a share of property in a tenancy in common is often called an *undivided share*. Given that each tenant in common has a quantifiable — if as of yet an undivided — share in the property, the right of survivorship does not apply to a tenancy in common. This undivided share in the property is not destroyed by the death of the tenant in common and can be passed on by the tenant in common to his successors by will or as governed by the rules of intestacy.

It is not necessary that tenants in common take equally, though they will often hold in equal shares. For example, Ian, David, Gerry and Martin co-own a property as tenants in common in equal shares. It follows that each of the co-owners has a quarter share of the property as a whole; no individual has a right to a certain quarter of the property. If, for example, Ian dies and it is provided that his property be divided among Paul and Don equally then the tenancy in common operates with David, Gerry and Martin holding notional quarter shares and Paul and Don holding notional one-eighth shares.

In the above, there is clearly unity of possession. This is the only unity that is required for a tenancy in common. It is therefore permissible for tenants in common to hold different interests in the property as there is no need for unity of interest. It is not necessary for the tenants in common to acquire their interest from the same conveyance or will, as there is no need for unity of title. And the interest of each tenant in common does not need to vest at the same time, as there is no need for unity of time. As regards unity of possession, it must be noted that if the co-owned land is producing an income in the form of profits, that income must be shared proportionally among the tenants in common.

Creation of a joint tenancy or tenancy in common

All four unities are essential to the creation of a joint tenancy and the lack of any one of them will prevent the creation of a joint tenancy. Nevertheless, even if the four unities are present, it must be noted that there may be an equitable presumption against a joint tenancy. The application of this presumption is demonstrated below. On the other hand, the successful creation of a tenancy in common needs only the unity of possession, even if a certain degree of unity of interest, time and title is present. If there is no unity of possession then neither a joint tenancy nor tenancy in common is created and separate ownership rights are said to exist between the grantees of the conveyance.

The common law has traditionally presumed that, wherever two or more persons are together entitled to possession of property, a joint tenancy exists. There was one very practical reason for this presumption. In a joint tenancy the right of survivorship applies and inevitably the number of joint tenants is reduced until such time as only one remains as the sole owner of the property. In a tenancy in common, however, each tenant has the right on death to pass his 'undivided' share on to his successors in title. It follows that, in the latter, ownership of the property may be continuously fragmented. This may lead to conveyancing difficulties. For example, in the sale of land, which is subject to a tenancy in common, not alone must the identity of the various tenants in common be established — meaning that the title of the individual tenant in common must be investigated — but also the consent of every tenant in common must be obtained. This can be a difficult, time-consuming and expensive task, and so the common law presumes in favour of a joint tenancy.

However, this presumption can be rebutted; first, by use of *words of severance*; second, the courts acting in their equitable jurisdiction may modify the application of the presumption; and, third, both common law and equity can act to sever the joint tenancy wherein severance is said to be the conversion of a joint tenancy into a tenancy in common.

Words of severance

At common law, the presumption is that a disposition of property in favour of two or more people together entitled to possession of that property, created a joint tenancy. However, if the disposition expressly directs that the grantees are to take as tenant in common, this direction would be effective. Equally, the presumption of a joint tenancy may be rebutted where, on the court's interpretation of the scheme of the disposition as whole, the actual intention of the grantor to dispose of a tenancy in common is implicitly indicated; see further *Bray v Jennings* (1902) 36 ILTR 6 and *Re Gray* (1927) 61 ILTR 65.

In their construction of the disposition as a whole, the courts will be alerted where the intention of the grantor suggests that the ownership of the property be based on a division of shares. Such an intention would be inconsistent with a joint tenancy and may be indicative of a tenancy in common. To assist them in this task the courts have noted that the use of phrases such as 'equally'; 'share and share alike'; 'to be divided between' and 'respectively' can be viewed as words of severance indicating the creation of a tenancy in common; see further *Lambert v Browne* (1871) IR 5 CL 218; *Mill v Mill* (1877) IR 11 Eq 158; *Crozier v Crozier* (1843) 3 Dr & War 373 and *Re Wallis's Trusts* (1888) 23 LR Ir 460.

Equity's preference for a tenancy in common

As noted in the first chapter, the concept of equity is based largely on tempering the occasional harshness of the common law. Equity was developed to present remedies and alternatives in situations where the common law presented none, or at least in situations where the common law's resolution was inflexible and unsuitable. However, equity cannot alter common law rules; its can merely soften their application. Remember the maxim *Equity follows the common law*; equity supplements but does not supplant the common law.

As regards co-ownership, equity regularly operates in the following manner. Equity views the right of survivorship, which operates in a joint tenancy, as being crudely and unfairly based on the principle of 'survival of the fittest'. Thus, in their equitable jurisdiction, the courts have argued that the benefits of ownership of property should not be accrued merely on the grounds of longevity: 'If I outlive the rest of the joint tenants, eventually I will end up as the sole owner of the property.' Generally, equity is said to 'lean against' joint tenancies. The alternative presented by equity is to split the ownership of the property into legal and equitable (beneficial) ownership. Thus, at law, the parties take the property as joint tenants but, in equity, they are said to hold that property on trust for themselves as tenants in common.

Equity uses this mechanism, thus leaning against joint tenancies, in three particular scenarios:

- where there are unequal contributions to the purchase money
- where there are joint business undertakings
- in the case of mortgage loans.

Unequal contributions to the purchase money

Where the purchasers of property provide the purchase money in unequal shares, there is an equitable presumption that they take the property as tenants in common in shares proportionate to their respective contributions. Equity imposes this presumption by means of a trust; see further *O'Connell* v *Harrison* [1927] IR 330. Accordingly, if one of the co-owners dies, the survivors take the whole legal interest but must hold a proportionate part of the property on trust for the co-owner's successors in title. If the purchase money was contributed equally, the presumption is that the co-owners take as joint tenants.

Joint business undertaking

Equity presumes that land, acquired by partners as part of the assets of their partnership, should be taken as having been acquired on the basis of a tenancy in common. Again, equity feels that the strict application of the right of survivorship would be inconsistent with the partnership relationship. This presumption applies irrespective of whether the partners have contributed equally to the acquisition of the land; see further *Hawkins* v *Rogers* [1951] IR 48, *O'Dwyer* v *Cafolla* [1949] IR 210 and *Meagher* v *Meagher* [1961] IR 96.

Since *McCarthy* v *Barry* (1859) 9 Ir Ch R 377, the presumption can be taken to extend to most joint business undertakings and applies whether or not any formal partnership has been entered into by the parties concerned.

Mortgage loans

Where two or more persons acquire an interest in land by lending money on mortgage, there is a presumption in equity that these persons are tenants in common. Two principles seem to underlie this presumption: 1. It is the nature of a mortgage transaction that each lender intends a return on that which he has lent; 2. the right of survivorship is seen to be inconsistent with the commercial nature of the transaction; see further *Steeds* v *Steeds* (1889) 22 QBD 537.

It must be remembered that all three of the above presumptions are rebuttable. For example, as regards unequal contributions to the purchase price, the equitable presumption of a tenancy in common may be rebutted by construing the scheme of the acquisition as a whole; see further *Fleming* v *Fleming* (1855) 5 Ir Ch R 129 and also *Reilly* v *Walsh* (1849) 11 Ir Eq R 22, where the presumption that partnership assets are held in tenancy in common was rebutted.

Severance of a joint tenancy

The common law did not need equity to remind it of the occasional unfairness of the operation of the right of survivorship in a joint tenancy. Thus, allowance was made for the severance of a joint tenancy wherein severance is simply the conversion of a joint tenancy into a tenancy in common. Severance can occur by alienation, the acquisition of a further interest, unlawful killing or mutual agreement.

Alienation

If one of the joint tenants gifts or sells his interest, that is, he alienates his interest to a third party, then the joint tenancy's unity of title is destroyed, resulting in severance. This is because the donee or purchaser derives his rights under a separate title from the remaining joint tenants; see further *Connolly* v *Connolly* (1866) 17 Ir Ch R 208 and *Re Armstrong* [1920] 1 IR 239.

The alienation must occur by way of an inter vivos transaction, as it is a fundamental principle of co-ownership that the courts will not allow a will to defeat the right of survivorship inherent in a joint tenancy.

The acquisition of a further interest

If one of the joint tenants acquires an interest in the property after the joint tenancy has come into existence then a severance will occur. This is because the unity of interest is destroyed; see further *Flynn* v *Flynn* [1930] IR 337.

For example, in a grant of land 'To David and Ian for life as joint tenants, remainder to Gerry in fee simple', if Ian acquires Gerry's fee simple, this purchase will sever the joint tenancy for life held by Ian with David, as it destroys their original unity of interest. The result is that David holds a half-share for life in the property as a tenant in common with Ian. Ian's half-share merges with his newly acquired fee simple. Thus, when David dies, Ian, or his successors in title, become the sole owners of the property.

Unlawful killing

A rule of forfeiture applies in a situation where a joint tenant unlawfully kills another so as to deprive the surviving joint tenant of the benefit of survivorship; see further *Re K (deceased)* [1986] 1 Ch 180. This is based on the maxim *A wrongdoer should not profit from his wrong*. In applying this maxim, equity, operating on its principle of unjust enrichment, severs the joint tenancy to prevent the surviving tenant from profiting from his own crime. In practice equity carries out this principle by allowing the legal title of the guilty joint tenant to vest by survivorship but holding that the beneficial interest be held by the killer on constructive trust for the deceased's estate. There is no Irish precedent on this area of the law; see further *Cleaver v Mutual Reserve* [1892] 1 QB 147 (Eng); *Schobelt v Barber* (1966) 60 DLR (2d) 519 (Can) and *Rasmanis v Jurewitsch* (1969) 70 SR (NSW) 407 (Aus).

Mutual agreement

A mutual agreement among joint tenants that henceforth they are to hold as tenants in common will amount to severance, and equity will give effect to such a contract; see further *Williams v Hensman* (1861) 1 John & Hem. 546. The joint tenants need not even formalise the agreement, as equity may infer such an intention from their conduct; see further *Harris v Harris* (1868) IR 3 CL 294, *Re Wallis's Trusts* (1889) 23 LR IR 460 and *Burgess v Rawnsley* [1975] Ch 429.

Determination of joint tenancies and tenancies in common

Severance of a joint tenancy does not put an end to the co-ownership of the property; it merely converts the joint tenancy to a tenancy in common. Actual determination of the co-ownership of the property may occur in three ways:

- sale
- partition of the property
- the union of the property in a sole tenant.

Sale

All the co-owners must agree to the sale (or mortgage) of the co-ownership property. The purchaser then receives the property free from the rights of the tenants. It must be noted that the co-ownership ends only as regards the property itself, as the co-ownership arrangement continues in the administration of the proceeds of the sale; see further *Byrne v Byrne*, 18 January 1980, High Court, McWilliam, J.

Partition

Partition is simply the physical division of the property into portions over which individual co-owners have exclusive rights and as it ends the unity of possession it results in the determination of the co-ownership.

The co-owners may voluntarily agree to put an end to their co-ownership and to partition the property in an agreed manner. As per Section 3 of the Real Property Act 1845, this voluntary partition must be effected through the execution of a deed. If one of the joint tenants or tenants in common refused to consent to the above, the other co-owners had no common law rights to force the partition on the dissenter. However, various statutory provisions, beginning in 1542 with legislation of Irish Parliament, empowered the courts to order partition. This 1542 Act was rendered obsolete in the jurisdiction by the Statute Law Revision (Pre-Union Irish Statutes) 1962. Nevertheless, there is an argument that in utilising Section 2(1) of the 1962 Act's recognition of existing principles of law and equity, an order of partition may be made under the court's general equitable jurisdiction; see further Murphy, J., in *O'D v O'D*, 18 November 1983, High Court and (more positively) Barr, J., in *CF v FF* [1987] ILRM 1.

From a practical point of view, the partition of property may be difficult. For example, if three persons have the joint tenancy of a house, how do you physically divide the property in three? Partition Acts of 1868 and 1871 circumvented this problem by permitting the sale of the property as followed by the division of the proceeds; see further *AL v JL*, 27 February 1984, High Court, Finlay, P., and *First National Building Society v Ring* [1992] 1 IR 375.

Union in a sole owner

In the case of a joint tenancy, the right of survivorship will eventually result in the property vesting in a sole survivor. Moreover, both joint tenancies and tenancies in common can be determined by one party buying out the interests of the others.

Further reading

Coughlan, P., *Property Law*, 2nd edn. Dublin: Gill & MacMillan, 1998, Chapter 8.
Lyall, A., *Land Law in Ireland*, 2nd edn. Dublin: Round Hall Sweet & Maxwell, 2000, Chapter 16.
Wylie, J., *Irish Land Law*, 3rd edn. Dublin: Butterworths, 1997, Chapter 7.

Self-test

In reviewing co-ownership, concentrate and elaborate on the following areas:

1. The four unities.

    Note in particular that a joint tenancy requires the presence of the four unities before it can be said to exist. While the four unities can also be present in the case of a tenancy in common, only that of the unity of possession is essential.

2. Equity's preference for a tenancy in common.

    What is meant by *Equity leans against joint tenancies*? How and when does equity lean against joint tenancies in favour of tenancies in common?

3. Compare the severance of a joint tenancy with its determination.

7
REGISTRATION

In Ireland, two main systems of registration exist in relation to land:

- the registry of deeds system (operated by the Registry of Deeds since 1708)
- the registration of title system (operated by the Land Registry since 1892).

Both registries are under the administrative control of the Registrar of Deeds and Title. The key objective of both systems is security of title.

It is important to note that the two systems are generally mutually exclusive in relation to the same estate in land. As will be explained and demonstrated, the registration of deeds system should gradually be replaced as the registration of title system extends. Accordingly, the latter system is of central importance in Irish land law.

Generally, it is said that the Registry of Deeds provides for the registration of *documents* dealing with land whereas the Land Registry provides for the registration of the *ownership* of land. A search of the Registry of Deeds will only give a list of the transactions concerning the land in question, whereas the ownership of estates in land is recorded or 'mirrored' in the files of the Land Registry. Therefore, if this option is available, it is much simpler to investigate title to land under the Land Registry system.

Registration of deeds: the Registry of Deeds

The key to both registries is security of title. Where a person seeks to purchase land, they should ordinarily investigate the vendor's title to the property. If the title to the property has been registered with the Land Registry, the mechanisms of the registration of title system apply. If title to the land has not been registered, as is the case with most urban land in Ireland, the vendor must produce the title deeds as proof of his right to sell. It is vital that the purchaser (or his agent) investigate these title deeds as they may disclose the existence of the rights of others, which the purchaser must respect. In other words, as was outlined in Chapter 1, the owner of land can create a variety of successive estates and interests (both legal and equitable) in his property so as to give various persons rights over that land. It follows that issues of priority may arise. The traditional rules for determining priority as between competing interests (mainly revolving around the equitable doctrine of notice) can be supplanted through use of the registration of deeds system, which was established by the Registration of Deeds Act 1707.

The registration of deeds system applies to interests in land, whether legal or equitable, arising under deeds, conveyances or wills. Registration of such documents is voluntary but where such a written disposition is effected, priority can be secured by registering a *memorial* (a summary document) at the Registry of Deeds, as certain advantages are enjoyed by a registered deed. Though registration of a memorial of a deed in no way guarantees the validity of the deed, as a general rule, a registered deed will prevail over an unregistered deed, irrespective of which came first in time and of the nature created by the registered deed; see Section 5 of the 1707 Act. Registered deeds take priority according to the order of their registration; see Section 4 of the Act.

The deed itself does not have to be lodged with the Registry of Deeds and a memorial will suffice. A memorial is simply a summary of the deed or conveyance. Under Section 6 of the Act, and in order to register the memorial, it must be signed and sealed by one of the parties to the transaction and be witnessed by two witnesses, at least one of whom was also a witness to the execution of the deed or conveyance itself. Under Section 7 of the 1707 Act, the memorial must contain the following basic information:

- the date of the document
- the name, addresses and occupations of all parties including witnesses to the documents
- a geographical description of the land affected by the document.

Notwithstanding the above, the registration of deeds system does not entirely displace the equitable doctrine of notice as a means of determining the priority of competing interests. First, as registration is not compulsory, there can still be a dispute between two unregistered dispositions, which must be resolved on the basis of the equitable rules. Second, the registration of deeds system depends on the registration of a memorial of a deed; thus, registration will be impossible if the interest in question is created independently of any deed or document. Finally, the courts are unwilling to allow the legislation to be used as an instrument of fraud. As a result, they reintroduced a limited version of the equitable doctrine of notice. If, when he acquire his own interest, a person has actual or imputed notice of a prior interest, he will not be permitted to gain priority for his subsequent interest by registering it first; see further *Agra Bank Ltd* v *Barry* (1874) LR 7 HL 135. It seems, however, that constructive notice will not suffice to trigger the reintroduction of the doctrine of notice; see further *O'Connor* v *McCarthy* [1982] IR 161.

N.B. The registration of deeds system in no way provides for the registration of land ownership, it merely establishes a means by which an estate or interest created by a registered deed or conveyance can take priority over another written disposition which has not been registered or which was registered at a later date. Searches in the Registry of Deeds can inform as to certain dispositions that were entered into in respect of that land but may reveal little as to the ownership of the land. In any event only a memorial of the deed or conveyance is lodged. To appreciate the precise effect of the disposition, the deed or conveyance itself would have to be examined. The registration of title system, however, provides for a central register where the ownership of freehold and leasehold estates is recorded. Once land is brought within this system, all subsequent transfers have to be effected in the prescribed manner and recorded on the register.

Registration of title: the Land Registry

The registration of title system was established in Ireland by the Local Registration of Title (Ireland) Act 1891. The 1891 system was established in parallel to the great land purchasing schemes of that time. While one of the objectives of this system of registration was to simplify the investigation of title to land, it was also recognised that:

> Public money ... had been advanced on the security of holdings, and it became a matter of public and financial importance that the title to those holdings should be kept clear from doubt and complication. (*Re Keogh* [1896] 1 IR 285, p. 294)

The result of the 1891 Act was that all land bought under the various land purchasing schemes had to be registered in the Land Registry and all subsequent dealing with the freehold title of that property had to be, and continues to be, recorded under this registration system. This has greatly simplified the conveyance of most agricultural land in Ireland, though the title to urban land remains complicated and largely the remit of the Registry of Deeds.

The Registration of Title Act 1964 amended the 1891 Act in the Republic of Ireland. The Act came into operation on 1 January 1967. For administrative purposes, the Land Registry is organised on a geographic basis. The central office of the Land Registry comprises four constituent offices, three in Dublin and one in Waterford. The Waterford office, for example, holds the registers for counties Carlow, Cork, Kerry, Kilkenny, Laois, Limerick, Offaly, Tipperary, Waterford and Wexford. In addition, there are 24 local offices based in the Circuit Courthouse in every county other than Dublin and Waterford. These local offices are under the management of a County Registrar.

The 1964 Act provides for the maintenance of three registers detailing freehold interests, leasehold interests and incorporeal hereditaments. According to section 31(1) of the 1964 Act, the basic principle of these records is that they are to be considered as conclusive evidence of the registered owner's title to the land. Sections 18 and 19 of the Act permit persons aggrieved by orders or decisions of the Registrar the right of appeal to the High Court or Circuit Court. Furthermore, under Section 32 of the Act, the High Court may order rectification of the register on the grounds of fraud or mistake. Any person suffering loss by reason of an official error in registration is entitled to compensation from the State, as per Section 120 of the Act.

To ensure that mistakes are kept to a minimum, the latest available Ordnance Survey maps are kept in the offices of the Land Registry. Each relevant parcel of land has a separate folio or file, which is cross-checked against the local map. This folio is divided into three parts. First, the land itself is described and cross-referenced with the registry map by means of a plan reference number. This cross-reference would normally include notes relating to easements, mines, minerals and boundaries. All properties in respect of which a title is registered must be depicted on a Land Registry map. The second section contains entries of the name, description and address of the owner or owners. Finally, there is a section devoted to any additional burdens, which may be on the land, for example, a mortgage or lease.

New folios may be created on foot of applications for first registration of title or subdivisions of existing folios. Existing folios may be updated on foot of applications lodged in the Registry. These applications could include transfers of registered property, mortgages and leases, or releases of existing burdens. The original folios and maps are maintained in the offices of the Land Registry. Duplicates of the folios (but not the maps) are kept in various local offices located in the Circuit Court offices of each county except Dublin and Waterford. Indexes of (i) the names of registered owners linking the name with the relevant folio number and (ii) the lands linking the plan number on the map with the corresponding folio number, are also maintained in the central offices of the Land Registry. Duplicates are kept in each relevant local office. The folios, maps and indexes and the duplicate folios and names index are available for public inspection and copying, in accordance with Section 107 of the 1964 Act.

There are three methods by which land can come within the registered land system. First, as per Section 23, an order may be made designating any local authority area as a compulsory registration area. Counties Carlow, Laois and Meath were so designated in 1970. Thereafter in these areas any transfer of freehold land necessitates the registration of that land, otherwise the transfer runs the risk of being declared void, as per Sections 24 and 25 of the Act. Second, and again under Section 23 of the Act, compulsory registration applies to land acquired by compulsory purchase by a state authority. Finally, apart from situations where registration is compulsory, the owner of land may make a voluntary application of registration. This seldom occurs — it is a time-consuming process — and is usually confined in urban areas to property developers who seek to divide a development site into a number of units, each of which will be covered by the same title deeds. It is interesting to note that, in England and Wales, registration has, on transfer, been made compulsory, as per the Registration of Title Order 1989.

Classes of title

On registration the owner is entitled to delivery of a land certificate — in effect a copy of the folio — indicating title, as per Section 28 of the Act.

There are different classes of title, each appropriate to the quality of title concerned. At first registration, the Registrar will attempt to fully assess and record the quality of title in question. This ensures that a person who is attempting to acquire an interest in registered land will be able to discover immediately the existence, for example, of any third-party rights that may affect the enjoyment of the land. Accordingly, an application for first registration must be accompanied by a statement of title summarising the basis of the applicant's claim to title, including all original deeds and documents pertaining to the land that are in the applicant's possession.

In accordance with Section 33 of the 1964 Act, a freehold owner may be registered with an absolute, qualified or possessory title. *Absolute* title is the most secure. If the title cannot be established as absolute to the satisfaction of the Registrar, for example, because it can be established for a limited time period only, it may be registered as a *qualified* title. This means that the title operates with the same effect as an absolute title except that it is subject to the estates or rights included in the qualification noted on the register; see further Section 39 of the 1964 Act.

If the Registrar is not satisfied that neither an absolute nor a qualified title would be appropriate, an applicant may still be registered with a *possessory* title. It is important to note that under Section 38(1), registration with a possessory title cannot prejudicially affect the enforcement of any right that is adverse to, or in derogation of, the title of the person registered as owner and subsisting or capable of arising at the time of registration. The typical example here is of a squatter who has been in adverse possession of land for less than the statutory 12-year limitation period (see further Chapter 8). The squatter can be registered as owner with possessory title but this does not prevent the person who is actually entitled to possession of the land from initiating legal proceedings to remove the squatter within the limitation period. Possessory title would however give the squatter greater certainty as regards his entitlement against persons other than the 'true' owner.

Similar classes of title, with similar effects, apply to leasehold estates; see further Section 40(1) of the 1964 Act. In addition, there is a fourth class of title for leaseholds called *good leasehold* title. This has the same effect as registration with absolute title, except that registration does not prejudicially affect the enforcement of any right adverse to, or in derogation of, the title of the lessor to grant the lease and no guarantee is offered as regards the title of the landlord; see further Section 45.

Finally, if evidence emerges, or if subsequent dealings, or even the passage of time, renders the existing class of title more secure, then the Registrar can ascribe a better class of title to the registered land. The Registrar may do this on his own initiative or subsequent to an application made by the registered owner or some other person who is entitled to the land; see further Section 50 of the 1964 Act.

Different classes of owners

A person may be registered as either a full or limited owner. For example, as regards freehold land, the owner may be registered as the full owner, that is, a fee simple estate, or as a limited owner of a settled estate, such as a fee tail or a life estate. The same applies to leasehold land — the owner is registered either as a full owner of the leasehold in possession or as a limited owner of a settled leasehold estate.

Burdens

The estate of the full or limited freehold owner of registered land is subject to any burdens that are registered as affecting the land (Section 37(3) of the Act) and any burdens that affect the land without need of registration (Section 72). A similar qualification applies to the leasehold interest of the registered owner as per Section 44(3) and Section 72 of the 1964 Act.

Thus, in effect there are two types of burden that concern registered land. The first category can be deemed registrable burdens and the second category are rights affecting land without registration, sometimes called *overriding interests*. A list of registrable burdens can be found in Section 69 of the 1964 Act and includes mortgages, easements and restrictive covenants. Registered burdens, which if unregistered would rank in priority according to the date of their creation, instead rank according to their order of their entry on the register, unless there is provision made to the contrary; see further Section 74 of the 1964 Act. It is important to note that if these rights are registered, they will be enforceable against someone who purchases the land for value; if they are not registered, a purchaser for value will take the land free of them. A person who receives a gift of land takes the land subject to whatever rights were enforceable against the person who gave him the land.

Burdens or rights affecting land without registration are detailed in Section 72 of the Act. These overriding interests include a diverse range of rights such as customary rights, public rights and rights acquired, or in the process of being acquired, under the doctrine of adverse possession. Implicit in Section 72 is the fact that there is recognition that it would simply be too time-consuming to register every possible right. The purchaser of registered land should, therefore, be aware that certain rights might affect the purchase even though they have not been registered. Indeed, Section 72(1)(j), which refers to rights of 'any person in actual occupation of land, or in receipt of the rents or profits thereof, save where, upon inquiry made of such persons, the rights are not disclosed', imports a modified version of the equitable doctrine of (constructive) notice into the registered land system (see reference in Chapter 1 to *Hunt* v *Luck* (1901)). This means that the purchaser of registered land must seek out any occupants of the land and make enquiries of them as to their rights; if the purchaser fails to do this, the rights of the occupant will bind him.

Trusts

Where registered land is held on trust, the trustees will be the registered owners and remain personally liable to the beneficiaries. Indeed, Section 37(4) of the 1964 Act specifically provides that if the registered owner holds land as a trustee, this does not affect his duties as a trustee. Section 44(4) applies the same principle to a leasehold interest held on trust.

Generally, trusts are not entered in the register and a purchaser for value of the registered land need not enquire as to whether the land is the subject of a trust, that is, a purchaser for value will take ownership of the land free from the trust; see further Section 92 of the Act.

However, under Section 72(1)(j), a purchaser of registered land may be bound by a trust affecting it if the beneficiary is in actual occupation of the property. Moreover, beneficiaries can protect their rights in the land through the use of cautions or inhibitions. Essentially, a caution prevents the trustee as the registered owner of the land from dealing with the land without prior warning being given to the beneficiaries; see further Section 97. As per

Section 98, an inhibition is a more permanent form of protection and is essentially a device that precludes any dealing with the property in question to the extent that the property is prevented from ever getting into the hands of a purchaser.

Transfer of registered land

The registered owner may transfer the registered land by using the appropriate prescribed form available under the Land Registry Rules 1972; for example, Form 10.2 is the form prescribed for the transfer of freehold by a full owner. Such a transfer does not of itself vest the land in the transferee. The owner of registered land is always the person recorded in the register; thus, until registration the transferee has only an 'equity' to be registered — in order to complete the transfer the transferee must have himself entered on the register as the new owner; see Section 51(2). Once registered, the transferee is entitled to delivery of the land certificate; see Section 51(3). If part only of the land is transferred, the Registrar may either allow the transferor to retain his certificate with an entry in it detailing the part transferred, or deliver to the transferor a new certificate as to the part retained; see Section 51(4).

As per Section 52 of the 1964 Act, on completion of the transfer by registration, the appropriate title vests in the transferee as if the transfer had been a conveyance by deed. If the transfer is a transfer for value, then the transferee takes subject to any burdens (both registrable burdens, as per Section 69 and those without registration, as per Section 72). Where the transfer is not a transfer for value, the transferee takes subject to all the above burdens and also all unregistered rights subject to which the transferor held the land transferred, for example, an undisclosed trust. As noted above, unregistered rights, such as an undisclosed trust, may be protected by cautions or inhibitions.

Exemption from and replacement of the Registry of Deeds

The general rule is that the two systems of title and deeds are mutually exclusive in relation to the same estate in land. In accordance with Section 116 of the 1964 Act, once the ownership of an estate or interest in land has been registered in the Land Registry, any deeds concerning the estate or interest executed after that date are exempted from registration in the Registry of Deeds. This means that a third party will not be able to gain priority over a written disposition of registered land by registering a memorial of the document under which he claims in the Registry of Deeds. From a practical point of view it also means that the registration of deeds system will remain in force until it is eventually displaced by the extension of the registration of title system, that is, until all parts of the State become subject to compulsory registration of title and all titles are eventually registered.

Conclusion

The Land Registry and Registry of Deeds in the Republic of Ireland now has an excellent website at http://www.irlgov.ie/landreg/. The site contains a concise introduction to the basic functions and objectives of the Land Registry and Registry of Deeds. It also includes online application forms for registration, as well as an update of fees and annual reports.

Further reading

Coughlan, P., *Property Law*, 2nd edn. Dublin: Gill & MacMillan, 1998, Chapters 5 and 7.

Lyall, A., *Land Law in Ireland*, 2nd edn. Dublin: Round Hall Sweet & Maxwell, 2000, Chapter 24.

Wylie, J., *Irish Land Law*, 3rd edn. Dublin: Butterworths, 1997, Chapters 21 and 22.

Self-test

Compare and contrast the system of registration of documents with that of registration of title. To what extent has the system of title registration provided a remedy for the defects in the earlier system?

8
ADVERSE POSSESSION

It is said that possession is nine points of the law and it is undoubtedly true that the importance of the concept of possession cannot be underestimated in Irish land law. The holder of an estate in land has a right to possess the land in question. The immediacy and length of this right will depend on the type of estate in question. The estate holder also has the right to occupy the property to the exclusion of others. In defending these rights against others, it is a fundamental principle of Irish land law that the estate holder need only demonstrate that he has a better right of possession than the other party. It is unnecessary for the estate holder to demonstrate that he is the owner of the property.

We can apply these basic principles to the following scenario: Ian owns property but does not occupy it. Gerry, who has no claim to the property, moves into the property without Ian's consent.

Gerry has entered into possession of the property without the owner's consent; therefore, Gerry is a trespasser and may be evicted by Ian, the true owner of the property. However, against others Gerry has possessory title, that is, Gerry has a right to the property based on possession. Under Irish land law, a person in possession without any claim of right (in our scenario, Gerry) is treated as having a right to the land which prevails against all except those who can demonstrate a superior title (in our case, Ian alone has superior title).

Furthermore, if Ian does not initiate an action to remove the Gerry within a stated, statutory limitation period then Ian, the paper owner of the property, may lose his legal right of action to defend his title and his title may be extinguished. The principle of limitation in its application to actions for the recovery of land obliges a person who has been unlawfully dispossessed of his land to bring an action to recover possession within the fixed period of time — usually 12 years — or have his title extinguished.

This situation regarding actions for the recovery of land is comparable to incidents where under statutes of limitations a person with a contractual right ceases to be able to enforce it after a period of years, usually six, from the date on which the cause of action accrued.

This acquisition of title to land by limitation is denoted by use of the term 'adverse possession', where adverse possession is taken to mean possession of land that is inconsistent with the title of the paper owner. The policies underlying this doctrine of adverse possession are twofold. First, the dilatory paper owner of land must recognise that rights of action to defend title to the land are limited in point of time and may be lost if not brought within the limitation period, for land is a scarce and valuable commodity and the title holder of the property has an obligation to use it or lose it!

Secondly, as per Lord St Leonard in *Dundee Harbour* v *Dougall* (1852) 1 Macq. 317, these limitation periods:

> ... have for their object the prevention of the rearing up of claims at great distances of time when evidences are lost; and in all well-regulated countries the quieting of possession is held an important point of policy.

Lord St Leonard is highlighting the fact that adverse possession operates under the principle of 'quieting', or clarifying, title to the land.

The limitation period

In the Real Property Limitation Act 1833, the period within which claims to recover the land must be brought was laid down for the first time. Section 2 of the Act gave the fixed period of limitation as 20 years. This was reduced to 12 years by the Real Property Limitation Act 1874. And under Section 13(2)(a) of the Statute of Limitations 1957 that 12-year period is the one now in force in Ireland.

Thus, in our example, if Ian does not assert his title by retaking possession of the land or initiating an action within the 12-year period laid out under the Statute of Limitations 1957, his title to the land will be extinguished. As Section 24 of the Statute of Limitations clearly states:

> ... at the expiration of the period fixed by this Act for any person to bring an action to recover land, the title of that person to the land shall be extinguished.

Usually, the 12-year limitation period begins to run from the date at which the cause of action accrues. Moreover, as per Section 18(1) of the Statute of Limitations 1957:

> No right of action to recover land shall be deemed to accrue unless the land is in [adverse] possession of some person in whose favour the period of limitation can run.

The paper owner of the property must either have given up possession of the property or been dispossessed of it and factual possession must have been taken up by another. Mere abandonment or vacancy of the land is not sufficient, because until someone else adversely possesses the property, the paper owner has no right of action against anyone, indeed, needs no right of action against anyone; see further *Fanning* v *Jenkinson*, 2 July 1997, High Court, Kinlen, J.

In addition, it is clear that a person who is in possession of the property under a lease or a licence cannot be deemed to be in adverse possession until the lease or licence has terminated; see further *Bellew* v *Bellew* [1983] ILRM 128 and Section 17 of the Statute of Limitations 1957.

Extension of the limitation period

It must be noted that the 12-year limitation period can be extended where at its commencement the paper owner of the property in question was unsound of mind, or an infant. Sections 47 and 48 of the Statute of Limitations 1957 state that in such cases the limitation period may be extended for six years after the ending of the disability, up to a maximum of 30 years from the accrual of the cause of action. Moreover, as per Section 71 of the Statute of Limitations, where a cause of action is based on or concealed by fraud the limitation period does not run until such time as the plaintiff could have reasonably discovered the fraud. However, where a claim is initiated against a bona fide purchaser for value without notice of fraud, the suspension of the time period does not apply.

It is also important to note, as regards the limitation period, that where the paper owner of the property has a limited estate or interest in the land, or is a mere tenant, the limitation period runs only against the paper owner and not against the person next entitled — the reversioner or remainderman. It is only on the determination of the prior interest that the limitation period begins to run against the person next entitled.

In fact, Section 15 of the Statute of Limitations 1957 states that if the prior interest is a life estate or a limited estate under a settlement, the person next entitled has 12 years from the accrual of action, or six years from the determination of the prior interest (whichever is the longer) to initiate an action. The same provision also notes that if the prior interest is a lease, the applicable limitation period for the landlord is 12 years from the determination of the lease.

Accumulation of the limitation period

The limitation period can run in favour of a series of squatters, provided that the property in question constantly remains in adverse possession; see further *Wallis* v *Howe* [1893] 2 Ch 545 and *Mount Carmel Investments Ltd* v *Thurlow* [1988] WLR 1078.

Interruption of the limitation period

A written or signed acknowledgement of the paper owner's title by the squatter interrupts the limitation period and the 12-year clock is 'rewound' to the start; see *Johnston* v *Smith* [1896] 2 IR 82, *Re Mitchell's Estates* [1943] IR 74, *Howard* v *Hennessy* [1947] IR 336 and Sections 50–60 of the 1957 Statute of Limitations.

Operation of the doctrine of adverse possession

The person in whose favour the limitation period runs is often referred to as a squatter. To establish that he is in adverse possession of the property it is necessary for the squatter to first demonstrate that he has factual possession of the property and, second, that he has the intention to possess the property to the extent that he excludes the true owner, and all other persons, from enjoyment of the estate or interest that is being acquired. The latter, intention-based, requirement is known as *animus possidendi* and may be negated by, among other factors, the written acknowledgement of the squatter of the paper owner's superior title.

The actions of the squatter must be definitive and clear to the extent that the reasonably alert owner should realise that his property is being adversely possessed; see further *Re Vernon's estate* [1901] 1 IR 1, *Doyle* v *O'Neill*, 13 January 1995, High Court, O'Hanlon, J., and *Griffin* v *Bleithin* [1999] 2 ILRM 182.

The key question is whether the squatter is acting in a manner consistent with the manner in which the true owner would act. For example, in the case of a farm, if the squatter repaired and maintained the land; if he used it systematically for grazing purposes and if he treated the entire land, as his own by banking the income from it, then on completion of the limitation period the paper owner's title will be extinguished; see further *Murphy* v *Murphy* [1980] IR 183. On the other hand, if the claim to adverse possession was based merely on the claimant's occasional walking on and gaming of the land, this may be deemed insufficient to establish adverse possession; see further *Hickson* v *Boylan*, 25 February 1993, Carroll, J.

In sum, casual usage of land is not consistent with the rights of a true owner and does not amount to a sufficient degree of possession to establish or infer adverse possession.

Future usage of the property

There is some debate about the establishment of adverse possession in the following instance. The paper owner does not occupy the land. He has no immediate use for the land, which is left vacant for the time being. Yet, the paper owner does intend to put the land to specific use at a later stage. For example, a local authority owns a strip of land near a major roadway. It has no immediate use for this plot and the plot is left, literally, at the side of the road. Yet, the local authority has a plan, to be enacted some time in the future, to use this plot of land in a major road-widening scheme. What if a farmer, whose land borders the roadway, begins to use this plot of land, for example, for parking his machinery, and even fences off the property to secure his machinery? Is the farmer entitled to adverse possession of the land if he consistently uses the land in such a manner until the expiry of the limitation period?

The leading case on this issue is *Leigh* v *Jack* (1879) 5 Ex D 264, the facts of which are analogous to the above. The squatter used the strip of land to store heavy materials, eventually fencing it off. However, it was held that the actions of the squatter did not take away from and were not inconsistent with the proposed, future intention of the paper owner. In *Buckinghamshire County Council* v *Moran* [1990] Ch 623, the English Court of Appeal retreated somewhat from the *Leigh* v *Jack* principle. In that case it was stated that, irrespective of the paper owner's future plans for the property, the squatter will establish adverse possession if it is shown that the squatter has factual possession of the property with the intention to possess the land to the exclusion of all others including the legal owner, that is, factual possession and *animus possidendi*. The contemporary English position is that it is not necessary for the squatter to perform acts that are inconsistent with the specific future plans of the landlord, in order to adversely possess the property; see further *London Borough of Hounslow* v *Minchinton* (1997) 74 P & CR 221.

In Ireland, a similarly principled retreat from Leigh v Jack occurred slightly earlier; see further Barron, J., in *Seamus Durack Manufacturing* v *Considine* [1987] IR 677. However, in *Cork Corporation* v *Lynch* [1995] 2 ILRM 598 and *Dundalk UDC* v *Conway*, 15 December 1987, High Court, Blayney, J., the courts were not as sympathetic towards the squatter. In the first mentioned case, the Cork Corporation acquired a plot of land with the intention that it should be used, at some future stage, as part of a road development scheme. The defendant owned a garage adjacent to the plot of land and he began to park cars on the plot. Over time he fenced off the plot and lay tarmac on it. Indeed, the defendant had sole and exclusive physical occupation of the plot for the duration of the limitation period. Nevertheless, on the basis of *Leigh* v *Jack*, Egan, J., held that adverse possession could not be established, as the defendant's actions, and indeed occupation, were not inconsistent with the intention of the local authority to use the land for its road development purpose.

Overall, the current state of Irish law on this matter is unclear and it is interesting to note that the Law Reform Commission has recommended that legislation should be enacted to ensure that the application of the doctrine of adverse possession in this regard is based on the straightforward definition of possession that is inconsistent with the title of the landowner, irrespective of possible future intentions of the paper owner towards the property; see further Land Law and Conveyancing Law: (1) General Proposals (LRC 30, 1989), pp. 26–7.

The quality and extent of rights acquired by the squatter

According to Section 24 of the Statute of Limitations 1957, on the expiration of the 12-year limitation period, the paper owner loses his right of action to recover the land and has his title extinguished. As a result, since the application of Section 24, the squatter is undoubtedly in a strong position in that he can no longer be sued or removed by the paper owner. However, Section 24 does not elaborate (nor does any other provision in the Statute of Limitations) on the actual rights acquired by the squatter.

Traditionally, it was thought that the squatter simply received whatever estate had been enjoyed by the dispossessed paper owner. This straightforward transfer was known as a parliamentary conveyance; see further Sir Edward Sugden in *Scott* v *Niron* (1843) 3 Dr & War 388, p. 407 and Parke, B., in *Doe d. Jukes* v *Sumner* (1845) 14 M & W 39, p. 42. The modern position somewhat rejects the *parliamentary conveyance* theory in that it doubts whether a full transfer operates in favour of the squatter. In the Irish case of *Rankin* v *McMurtry* (1889) 24 LR Ir 290, Holmes, J., argued:

> ... the title gained by such [adverse] possession, being limited by rights ... is clearly commensurate with the interest which the rightful owners have lost ...

As regards the adverse possession of freehold land, the distinction between the straightforward concept of parliamentary conveyance and subtler phrasing of 'commensurate with the interest that the rightful owners have lost', is minimal. For example, if the squatter dispossesses the paper owner of an absolute fee simple, then the squatter acquires all those benefits and rights associated with the largest estate known in land law. The squatter also receives any burdens associated with the estate, for example, easements. Similarly, if the squatter dispossesses the paper owner of a life estate, the squatter holds the land for the length of that life estate — the squatter's estate lasts until the death of the dispossessed owner as this is the interest commensurate with that which was lost by the rightful owner.

However, the movement away from the simplicity of the parliamentary conveyance caused significant difficulties where the squatter dispossesses a tenant. Under the parliamentary conveyance theory where, at the expiry of the limitation period the squatter dispossesses a tenant, the effect was similar to an assignment in that the original lessee was relieved of all his obligations under the lease and the squatter seamlessly took on these obligations. The landlord's position was unaffected and he could continue to enforce the terms of the lease on his 'new' tenant.

In brief, the primary advantage of the parliamentary conveyance in this regard was that the leasehold estate vested directly in the squatter. In *Tichborne* v *Weir* (1892) 67 LT 735, the English Court of Appeal rejected the above view. Though the squatter may dispossess the tenant, the Court held that the squatter does not acquire the tenant's estate.

It is suggested that in *Tichborne* the English Court of Appeal viewed the possession of the estate by the squatter as a 'hostile takeover' of the original agreement and that this 'takeover' should be barely acknowledged and positively discouraged. In *Tickner* v *Buzzacott* (1965) Ch 426, Plowman, J., noted that the landlord not only has the right to possession of the property on the natural expiry of the lease but also that he retains the right of re-entry for breach of condition. In *Fairweather* v *St Marylebone Property Co. Ltd* [1963] AC 510, the hostility of the English Courts towards the tenant-squatter manifested itself by the House of Lords holding that even though the tenant's title had been extinguished by the actions of the squatter, the tenant could still surrender the residue of his lease to the landlord. The landlord could then immediately recover possession of the property and even grant a new lease to the dispossessed lessee. In other words, the original landlord and tenant could collude, to their mutual benefit, so as to remove the squatter.

The *Fairweather* approach is open to criticism on two grounds. First, the squatter has over the 12-year period dispossessed the lessee and established adverse possession to the extent that the lessee cannot directly recover possession of the property from the squatter. If the dispossessed lessee has legally lost his right of recovery how then can the lessee have the capacity to give another — the landlord — the right to recover the property?; see further the dissenting judgement of Lord Morris, who cites the maxim *nemo dat quod non habet* — one cannot give what one does not have.

Second, the original basis for the promotion of the doctrine of adverse possession was to prevent 'the rearing up of claims at great distances of time'. It is submitted that the *Fairweather* scheme is not consistent with this policy.

Initially, the Irish Supreme Court took a more benign view of the squatter; see further *Perry v Woodfarm Homes Ltd* [1975] IR 104. In that case, a small plot of ground was held under a 999-year lease. In 1970, the lessee assigned his interest in the property to the defendants. A month later the defendants acquired the fee simple reversion. Thereafter, the defendants utilised the doctrine of merger — when two estates, a greater and lesser, become vested in the same person and in the same right without any intervening period between them, the lesser estate is merged in the greater. Thus, the defendants argued that in their case the lease (the lesser estate) was merged with the greater estate (the fee simple reversion); the defendants argued that the leasehold estate was now extinguished and that they now possessed the fee simple. The defendants duly registered their title to the freehold in the Land Registry and planned to develop the plot.

However, since 1955 the property had been in the exclusive possession of the plaintiff. In fact, the lessee's title was clearly extinguished by the plaintiff by 12 years' adverse possession. The plaintiff sought and was granted a perpetual injunction to restrain the defendants from developing the property.

The majority of the Supreme Court felt that, as the title of the tenant had been extinguished by adverse possession, the dispossessed tenant had no capacity to assign the lease to the defendants and merger could not therefore occur. The Supreme Court stated that the squatter had the right to possession of the property for the unexpired portion of the lease subject to the risk and possibility of forfeiture for breach of one or more of the covenants in the lease.

In theory then the status of the Irish squatter is slightly better than the English equivalent and so long as the squatter endeavours to perform the appropriate covenants, the lessor has no right to possession of the property. However, in practice, as the squatter was not privy to the original lease, he may be unaware of the precise details of the lease. The threat of forfeiture will therefore be constant.

Overall, the situation regarding adverse possession against lessees is unsatisfactory. This dissatisfaction can be traced to the demise of the application of the parliamentary conveyance theory. It is suggested that legislation should be enacted so that on the expiry of the limitation period the leasehold interest directly vests in the squatter to the extent that the squatter succeeds to all the rights and obligations of the dispossessed lessee under the lease; this is a limited statutory revival of the parliamentary conveyance.

Registration

As regards registered land, the paper owner's registered title is not automatically extinguished by virtue of adverse possession. Adverse possession of itself does not give the squatter the automatic right to be registered as owner in derogation of the registered owner's title. Section 49 of the Registration of Title Act 1964 provides that where a squatter has acquired an estate in registered land by adverse possession, he may apply for an order declaring his title and for the appropriate rectification of the register. In the rectification process, it is the practice of the Land Registry for registration to be made in the same folio as that of the dispossessed paper owner.

Finally, it must be noted that even if the squatter does not utilise Section 49 and does not register his interest, the squatter's interest, acquired by adverse possession, is not adversely affected in that it remains the overriding interest in the land, as per Section 72 of the 1964 Act. This means that the registered paper owner, and his successors in title will, irrespective of registration, hold the property subject to the rights of the squatter.

Conclusion

The doctrine of adverse possession has three components. First, there is the neglect of the paper owner towards his property. This could be evidenced by the property remaining vacant. Second, there is the factual possession of the property by the squatter. This could be evidenced by the squatter acting in a manner consistent with the ownership of the property. Lastly, there is *animus possidendi* — the apparent intentionof the squatter to exclude all others from the property, including the paper owner.

Further reading

Coughlan, P., *Property Law*, 2nd edn. Dublin: Gill & MacMillan, 1998, Chapter 12.
Lyall, A., *Land Law in Ireland*, 2nd edn. Dublin: Round Hall Sweet & Maxwell, 2000, Chapter 25.
Wylie, J., *Irish Land Law*, 3rd edn. Dublin: Butterworths, 1997, Chapter 23.

Self-test

The following are typical examples of exam questions. They focus on all the major issues such as factual possession, *animus possidendi* and the quality of rights acquired by the squatter. They also focus on minor issues such as the accumulation and interruption of the limitation period.

1. A wealthy local businessman, Mr Burns, leased Dunroamin, a property consisting of a house and two acres of land, to Ned in 1984 for a period of 20 years. Ned, a deeply religious man, was too preoccupied to make use of the property and it was left vacant for two years, during which Barney, the town drunk, made frequent use of the premises for shelter. In December 1986, a local publican, Moe, occupied the property and resided in the house until 1994, when he transferred the property over to Homer in exchange for a collection of beer mats. Homer has resided on the property since that date. However, in December 2000, Homer's wife, Marge, feeling sorry for Ned, convinced Homer to speak to Ned and remind him that the property did in fact belong to Ned. Mr Burns, meanwhile, wishes to build a sewage disposal plant on the site and has just demanded that Homer surrender possession to him immediately.

    Advise Homer.

2. In 1973, Caroline inherited a small house in the country from her aunt. She visited the property but did not want to live there, as her career was in the city. However, she decided to keep the house as a weekend retreat and ultimately as a retirement home. She asked her neighbour, Richard to 'keep an eye on' the house for her and gave him a spare key for emergencies.

    Due to pressure at work, Caroline never in fact bothered to go to the house at weekends, as she had intended. After a while, from about 1975, Richard began using the garden of the house as a vegetable patch. In 1978, he noticed that the grounds were becoming run down, and he carried out repairs, which cost him about £200. Included in the repairs was a new gate, which Richard kept locked with a padlock, of which he had the only key. He did not bother to tell Caroline about this, as she never got in touch with him. From 1979, Richard began to make use of the house itself, as accommodation for friends, and then as rented summer accommodation. He did not lock the gate at these times but kept the rent for himself.

In 1989, Richard sold his own land to Sid, and also gave him the key to Caroline's house. He told Sid that Caroline 'hadn't shown up for years' and 'could be dead for all he knew'. Sid continued to use the house and garden as Richard had done before him. In 2000, Caroline retired from work and turned up demanding the key.

Advise Sid.

9
SETTLEMENTS

In a general sense, 'settlement' may denote any disposition of any kind of property in favour of successive owners, usually with the motive of retaining the property in the family name. There are two basic types of settlement:

- trusts — in which the settlor leaves the property, which can be realty or personalty or both, to trustees to be held for the benefit of family members.
- strict settlements — which do not involve the use of any trust, at least not in the original disposition of the land and, unlike the trust concept, they are confined to realty — land — only.

This chapter concentrates on strict settlements. A strict settlement was a traditional common law device used by families, particularly the landed gentry, to ensure that land remained within the family name for successive generations. Typically, land would be strictly settled by use of limited freehold estates such as the fee tail and the life estate. For example, a landowner may have disposed of his property to his eldest son for life and thereafter to that son's eldest son in tail. The settlement may also have detailed ways in which other members of the immediate family would have to be provided for, for example, the widow being supported by a maintenance annuity while the other children being compensated with a capital sum, known as a *portion*.

Consider the position of the eldest son who obtains the immediate life estate. First, he must pay off the other children and support the surviving spouse, thus, incurring considerable expense. Second, in raising this money it must be remembered that the estate received by the eldest son was of dubious commercial value. No lease granted by the life owner was effective after his death and his estate would often be considered too precarious to be sufficient security for a mortgage. Indeed, such would be the restrictions that the land would be rendered virtually inalienable. In practice, this meant that the person in immediate possession of the land had neither the power nor the incentive to develop the land. Moreover, this potential mismanagement of the land was exacerbated by the fact that the strictness of the settlement prevented the land from entering the open property market.

Reform was needed and this came in the form of legislation — the Settled Land Acts 1882–90.

Settled Land Acts 1882–90

Section 2(3) of the Settled Land Act 1882 defines settled land for the purposes of the legislation as:

> land, and any estate or interest therein, which is the subject of a settlement.

The key term 'settlement' is defined by Section 2(1) of the same Act:

> Any land, or estate or interest in land, stands for the time being limited to it in trust for any persons by way of succession.

In short, any document creating a succession of interests in land can be deemed a settlement.

The basic objective of the legislation is to give the limited owner — the immediate possessor of the land — greater powers to deal with the settled land, including the power to sell the land. Under the Acts, the limited owner is called the *tenant for life*. The powers and functions of the tenant for life are central to the operation of the legislation.

Tenant for life

Section 2(5) of the 1882 Act defines a tenant for life as:

> the person who is for the time being, under a settlement, beneficially entitled to possession of settled land, for his life.

In practice, the tenant for life is usually a person with a life estate in immediate possession.

The tenant for life has extensive statutory powers to deal with the land including the power to sell, exchange, lease and mortgage the land. However, before discussing these powers individually, it is necessary to make two fundamental points about the framework in which the tenant for life operates.

First, Section 53 of the 1882 Act is quite clear that in exercising the above powers the tenant for life is under a fiduciary obligation to all other persons who have an interest in the settlement. The tenant for life must act under the bona fides of a trustee. However, the courts will allow the tenant for life, as it does with all trustees, a certain measure of discretion in the exercise of his powers. Courts may be reluctant to intervene unless it can be shown that the transaction undertaken by the tenant for life materially harms the other beneficiaries' interests under the settlement.

A good example of this principle in action is the case of *Wheelwright* v *Walker* (1883) 23 Ch D 752. The tenant for life attempted to sell the house in question. The transaction was apparently motivated by the fact that the house was too large for his needs and if he could sell the house he could move into a smaller, more economical house and have money left over to increase his comfort in his old age; at the time he was 70. The plaintiffs objected to this motive, which they argued selfishly ignored their future interests under the settlement. The court held that it had no power to interfere with the tenants for life's power to sell, provided the requirements of the Settled Land Acts were complied with. Despite the evident selfishness of his motive, the court was mindful of the fact that the aim of the legislation was to free up land from the fetters of settlement. However, in this instance the court heard evidence that the plaintiffs had offered to buy the house and that not only had the tenant for life been unwilling to sell it to the plaintiffs at this fair market price but that the tenant for life had offered to sell the house to another for a lower price. Given this evidence the court stopped the sale.

Second, under Section 50 of the 1882 Act a tenant for life cannot assign his powers to another. Similarly the settlor cannot, under Section 51, do anything to oust, curtail or hamper the powers as exercised by the tenant for life. A good example of this is the case of *Re Fitzgerald* [1902] IR 162. In that case the tenant for life had a life interest in a house but there was a condition precedent of residence. The tenant for life wanted to exercise his power of sale but it was argued that this would violate the residency requirement of the original settlement. The court permitted the sale, as under Section 51 the tenant for life's powers cannot be curtailed.

It must be noted that Section 56 of the 1882 Act reiterates this point and goes on to state that where the provisions of a settlement and the provisions of the Acts conflict, the provisions of the Acts relating to the powers of the tenant for life must prevail. Finally, Section 57 of the 1882 Act states that nothing in the Acts prevents the settlor from conferring on the tenant for life any powers additional to or larger than those conferred by the Act.

Designated statutory powers

Having established the framework in which the tenant for life operates under, it is now necessary to discuss his specific statutory powers. In a general sense, the tenant for life has the power of sale, lease, mortgage, improvement and various other miscellaneous powers.

Sale

Section 3 of the Settled Land Act 1882 confers on the tenant for life the power to sell or exchange the settled land or any part thereof. Under Section 4 the tenant for life must exercise his power so that:

> Every sale shall be made at the best price that can be reasonably obtained.

The power to sell the land is indicative of the key objective of the legislation, which is to give the person designated as the tenant for life greater powers of dealing with the settled land than he would otherwise have. Therefore, as in the case of a sale, provided the proper procedures are observed the purchaser obtains a fee simple freed and discharged from all the other estates or interests which may have been attached to the land under the original settlement.

One of these proper procedures is that after the sale the money raised, which is called the *capital money*, is not given to the tenant for life as income but is paid to persons known as the *trustees to the settlement*. The role played by the trustees will be discussed later, suffice to say that in order to prevent the potential squandering of the capital money these trustees receive it and may then invest it, subject to Sections 21 and 22 of the 1882 Act. This process whereby the land is sold free of all encumbrances created by the settlement, which thereupon are transferred to the capital money fund, is known as *overreaching*.

Finally, as regards the power of sale (and also the power of the tenant for life to exchange, lease and mortgage) under Section 45 of the 1882 Act the tenant for life must give at least one month's notice of his intention to sell to the aforementioned trustees of the settlement. However, Section 45(3) expressly provides that:

> A person dealing in good faith with the tenant for life is not concerned to inquire respecting the giving of any such notice ...

Moreover, under Section 54 such a bona fide purchaser shall, as against all other parties entitled under the settlement, be conclusively taken to have given the best price that could reasonably be obtained by the tenant for life, and to have complied with all the requirements of the Acts.

Lease

Under Section 6 of the Settled Land Act 1882 the tenant for life has various powers to lease the settled land. Such a lease will survive for its full term despite the death of the tenant for life. The Act lays down maximum limits on the length of the leases, for example, 99 years for building leases, 60 years for mining leases and 35 years for other leases.

In operating this power, the tenant for life must abide by several conditions laid out in Section 7 of the 1882 Act. The first four subsections of that provision can be summarised as follows:

- Every lease shall be made by deed and may be made to take effect in possession not later than 12 months after its date.
- Every lease shall reserve the best rent that can be reasonably obtained.
- Every lease shall contain a covenant by the lessee for payment of the rent and condition of re-entry on the rent not being paid within a time therein specified not exceeding 30 days.
- A counterpart of every lease must be executed by the lessee and delivered to the tenant for life; though execution and delivery of same by the tenant for life shall be sufficient evidence that this has been done.

Similarly to the power of sale, one month's notice of an intention to lease must be given by the tenant for life to the trustees as per Section 45 of the 1882 Act. Furthermore, as per the power of sale and the bona fide purchaser, Section 45 and Section 54's bona fide protection applies to a lessee; see further *Gilmore* v *O'Connor Don* [1947] IR 462.

In addition to the general provisions of Sections 6 and 7, the Settled Land Act 1882 contains special provisions relating to building and mining leases. These special provisions are contained in Sections 8 and 9 respectively.

Mining leases are an interesting exception to the general rule that the rent reserved in leases for settled land is treated as part of the tenant for life's income from the land; see further *Re Wix* [1916] 1 Ch 279. In the circumstance of a mining lease the capital value of the land will evidently be diminished by the mining and extraction of the ore, hence, it is provided by Section 11 of the 1882 Act that part of the rent raised should be set aside as capital money. In effect, this rent is set aside as compensation for the damage done to the estate. The remainder goes, as usual, to the tenant for life as income; see further *Re Hall* [1916] 2 Ch 488 and *Re Bruce* [1932] 1 Ch 316.

Mortgages

The Settled Land Acts 1882–90 do not confer wide powers of mortgaging settled land for fear of binding the interests of successive owners. To this end, the tenant for life can usually mortgage only his own interest under the settlement or operate within the particular limited circumstances laid out in Section 18 of the 1882 Act.

Even in such statutorily permitted cases both the legislature and the courts are acutely aware that the exercise of such statutory powers of mortgaging by the tenant for life may override the interests of the other beneficiaries under the settlement. Accordingly, the statute provides that money raised in such instances is to be treated as capital money made payable to the trustees of the settlement. Moreover, the courts will intervene if it is clearly shown that the tenant for life is exercising his powers in this regard in a manner prejudicial to the interests of the other beneficiaries; see further *Hampden* v *Earl of Buckinghamshire* [1893] 2 Ch 531 and *Re Richardson* [1900] 2 Ch 778.

Improvements

A fourth power of the tenant for life concerns improvements. Improvements can generally be defined as expenditures over and above the daily running and maintenance of the land. The key question in this area of the law is whether the tenant for life is to pay for these improvements or whether they should be paid out of the capital money.

Section 25 of the 1882 Act contains an extensive list of works that may be executed by use of the capital money. Examples include the construction of buildings and drainage schemes. If the tenant for life wishes to have capital money devoted to these improvements he must, under Section 26 of the 1882 Act, submit a detailed scheme for approval by the trustees of the settlement.

Finally, under Section 28 of the 1882 Act, once improvements have been made under the Acts, the tenant for life and each of his successors in title under the settlement, is obliged out of his own funds to maintain the improvements. This area of law is discussed in detail in *Standing* v *Gray* [1903] 1 IR 49.

Miscellaneous

The Settled Land Acts confer various other miscellaneous powers on the tenant for life. For example, under Section 10(2) of the 1890 Act the 'principal mansion house' and its grounds may not be sold, exchanged or leased by the tenant for life without the consent of the trustees of the settlement or an order of the court. The aim here is to prevent against dispositions relating to that part of the settled land as might have some special sentimental value to other members of the family, which money cannot replace or compensate for. With this principle in mind similar restrictions apply to family heirlooms such as paintings, antiques or furniture. These latter restrictions are contained in Section 37 of the 1882 Act.

In summary, given the nature and extent of the powers outlined above, it is clear that the main control of the settled land is placed firmly in the hands of the tenant for life. This is obviously a risky thing to do since the tenant for life may have his own interests in mind when he chooses to exercise a statutory power. As the interests of future beneficiaries are also at stake, and to guard against an abuse of power, the Settled Land Acts created 'trustees of the settlement', who act in a supervisory capacity towards the settlement as a whole.

Trustees of the settlement

The role of the trustees of the settlement is to ensure, by and large, that the tenant for life in exercising his powers under the Acts does so for the benefit of the settlement as a whole. The task of the trustees is a delicate balancing act between regulating the significant powers given to the tenant for life by the Acts and not overly restricting the actions of the tenant for life. The latter would go against the key objective of the Acts, which is to free the land, and the immediate possessor of that land, from the fetters of the original settlement.

The Settled Land Acts clearly lay out the extent of supervision that needs to be taken on by the trustees. For example, in many dealings with the land the tenant for life must give the trustees prior notice of his intentions and the capital money raised on such transactions must be given directly to the trustees. Moreover, in certain instances, such as the proposed sale of the principal mansion house, it has been demonstrated that the tenant for life must obtain the express consent of the trustees before the transaction can take place.

Section 2(8) of the 1882 Act, as supplemented by Section 16 of the 1890 Act, identifies those who are to be considered trustees of the settlement. Under these provisions, those persons:

> ... who are by the settlement declared to be trustees thereof for the purposes of this Act, are for the purposes of this Act trustees of the settlement.

In other words, it is usual that the trustees will be expressly declared by the settlement itself. It is important to note that it is not sufficient simply to designate certain persons as 'trustees' or even as 'trustees of the settlement', they must be clearly appointed as trustees of the settlement for the purposes of the Settled Land Acts 1882–90.

Section 16 of the 1890 Act supplements the above. It provides that where no appropriate trustees are appointed by the settlement itself, trustees with a power of sale of other land that is subject to the same limitations as the settled land in question, will suffice. A simple example of this is that a settlement may include two farms but the trustees named were given power only to sell one of them. The effect of Section 16 of the 1890 Act is to make these trustees the trustees of the settlement as a whole.

If trustees of the settlement are not designated under the Acts, the courts may duly appoint trustees as per Section 38(1) of the 1882 Act.

Designated statutory powers

The trustees of the settlement fulfil their protective and supervisory role by means of the following.

Capital money

It is enshrined in the Acts that the tenant for life must respect the principle of overreaching. The proceeds from sales and mortgages must be given directly to the trustees of the settlement, as per Section 22 of the 1882 Act. This is mainly to prevent against the squandering of such capital monies by the tenant for life, principally on himself. Four technical points need to be made about this procedure.

First, unless the settlement itself authorises otherwise, the payment of the capital money must be paid to at least two trustees, as per Section 39 of the 1882 Act. Under Section 22(1) of the same Act, the purchaser has an option to advance the capital money either to these two trustees directly or to the court, whose power to receive such money is contained in Section 46 of the 1882 Act. A receipt issued by the trustees or the court is an essential part of any purchaser's title to settled land and lack thereof will be a fatal flaw towards title, particularly for the purposes of subsequent transactions relating to the land in question.

Under Section 22(2) the capital money paid to the trustees must be invested or applied by them in accordance with the direction of the tenant for life (or if no direction is given at their own discretion). Section 21 of the 1882 Act provides various methods by which the capital money can be applied, for example, for improvements to the land or invested in government securities or any other investment as authorised by the settlement itself.

In exercising his investment direction, the tenant for life is acting in a fiduciary position and, where the conduct of the tenant for life clearly harms the interests of the other beneficiaries under the settlement, the court will intervene, usually at the behest of the trustees of the settlement; see further *Re Hunt's Settled Estates* [1906] 2 Ch 11. Here, the tenant for life bought a lease lasting 60 years for £2,500 [€ 3,200]. The trustees of the settlement were notified as per Section 45 of the 1882 Settled Land Act and on inspecting the premises discovered it to be in a dilapidated state and worth about £1,000 [€1,270] less. The court permitted the trustees to ignore the tenant for life's investment direction. There was evidence that the tenant for life and the lessor were acting in collusion.

Similarly, where the investment plan of the tenant for life can be regarded as bad business sense, the trustees may have the investment direction quashed; see further *Re Somers* (1895) 11 TLR 567. The tenant for life in this case would only agree to lease a pub if the lessee would sign a covenant not to sell alcohol.

Where the loss is only speculative, the investment plan will not be interfered with by the court; see further *Thomas* v *Williams* (1883) 24 Ch D 558, in which the tenant for life wished to sell the settled land. It was argued that if the tenant for life delayed, the value of the land would probably increase due to the likely passing of a Bill of Parliament for the construction of a railway through the land in question. The court refused to uphold these arguments on the grounds of speculation and allowed the sale.

Notice

Most of the major powers conferred by the Acts on the tenant for life can only be exercised by his first giving notice to the trustees. This is provided for in Section 45 of the 1882 Act. The notice, which is one month in duration and usually sent by post, must, as per subsection 2 of Section 45, be given to at least two trustees. As demonstrated in the *Hunt* and *Somers* cases, the period of notice gives the trustees time to check out the actions of the tenant for life to investigate whether or not they materially harm the future beneficiaries under the settlement.

Consent

In certain instances, the tenant for life requires the consent of the trustees of the settlement before a transaction can be executed in full. For example, as regards the sale of the principal mansion house, the consent of the trustees is required under Section 10(2) of the 1882 Act. Similarly, under Section 35 of the same Act the consent of the trustees must also be obtained in the case of cutting and subsequently selling timber. Finally, under Section 37 consent must also be obtained before a family heirloom can be sold.

Miscellaneous

Apart from the above principal functions, the Acts confer certain miscellaneous functions on the trustees. An important example of such a function is contained in Section 60 of the 1882 Act. Under this provision it is provided that where the tenant for life is an infant, the trustees of the settlement may exercise the minor's statutory powers until he reaches the age of majority. Similarly, if the tenant for life wishes to purchase the land outright, the tenant for life must transfer his powers to the trustees who then negotiate the purchase price with him.

Conclusion

The proper operation of the Settled Land Acts revolves around the relationship between the tenant for life and the trustees of the settlement. It is evident from the objective and scheme of the Act that the tenant for life is the more influential party in that the trustees act in a supervisory capacity only. In addition, under Section 53 of the 1882 Act it is clear that the obligation to look after the interests of the other beneficiaries in exercising the statutory powers is placed firmly by the Acts on the tenant for life. In fact, it can be argued, with reference to Section 42 of the 1882 Act, that even if the trustees consider the actions of the tenant for life as improper they are under no obligation to bring an action against the tenant for life. Nevertheless, as a matter of sound practice, the trustees will take a more active role than that implied by Section 42. Indeed, why bother creating such a position if the trustees are merely going to 'rubberstamp' the actions of the tenant for life?

In sum, the critical relationship between the tenant for life and the trustees under the Settled Land Acts 1882–90 may be best analysed in the following context of Irish constitutional law. The trustees of the settlement are equivalent to the office of President; the tenant for life plays the role of the Taoiseach; the settled land in question is the State; the Settled Land Acts are equivalent to the Constitution and the people of Ireland are the other beneficiaries under the settlement. The President's role (trustees of the settlement) is largely ceremonial under the Constitution (Settled Land Acts 1882–90) and formalises many of the actions of the Taoiseach (tenant for life) who in effect runs the country (settled land) for our benefit with regard to the Constitution (Settled Land Acts 1882–90). While the President's role (trustees of the settlement) is largely passive and the people (the other beneficiaries) are usually able to protect their own interests, in certain circumstances, the President (as trustee of the settlement) can and should under the Constitution (Settled Land Acts 1882–90) be an important protector of the rights of the people.

Further reading

Coughlan, P., *Property Law*, 2nd edn. Dublin: Gill & MacMillan, 1998, Chapter 11.

Lyall, A., *Land Law in Ireland*, 2nd edn. Dublin: Round Hall Sweet & Maxwell, 2000, Chapter 14.

Wylie, J., *Irish Land Law*, 3rd edn. Dublin: Butterworths, 1997, Chapter 8.

Self-test

1. 'The obligation to look after the interests of the other beneficiaries in exercising the statutory powers is placed firmly by the Settled Land Acts 1882–90 on the tenant for life.'

    Discuss the merits of this statement in the context of the Acts as a whole.

2. Lord Halsbury, referring to the Settled Land Acts, 1882–90 in *Bruce* v *Ailesbury* [1892] AC 356, p. 361, observed:

    > ... the statute ... intended to release the land from the fetters of the settlement to render it a marketable article notwithstanding the settlement.

    Critically analyse the methods that the Settled Land Acts, 1882–90 employed in fulfilling the above intention.

10
SUCCESSION

There are three basic means of transferring property. First, there is an inter vivos transfer, which is where the owner is alive and he either sells or gifts his property to another. Second, property can transfer on the death of the owner; this is succession. And third, property can be transferred by means of a *donatio mortis causa*, which is a hybrid form of transfer entailing a gift made by a person while he is alive but in contemplation of and conditional upon his death.

This chapter will concentrate on the law of succession. There are two sets of rules governing the manner by which property can be disposed of on death — testate succession and intestate succession.

Testate succession, sometimes referred to as testamentary succession, arises where the owner, when alive, draws up a will laying out who is to receive his various items of property. There are four basic introductory points to be made about wills and testate succession.

1. A will need not be one single document. It may be a collection of documents, although invariably it is one single instrument with possibly an additional clarifying or amending document called a codicil.

2. The person who makes the will, known as the *testator* (male) or the *testatrix* (female), traditionally had considerable freedom of the testation in that he or she could virtually dispose of property to whomever or whatever they saw fit. This was the position under the old legislation governing wills, beginning in Ireland with the Statute of Wills 1634 and later the Wills Act 1837. However, in a welcome change and virtual codification of the law on succession, the Succession Act 1965 was enacted which, among other provisions, limited or qualified the freedom of the testator. Under the Act, specific provision was made for any surviving spouse and children of the testator.

3. As regards testamentary succession, it is a well-settled principle that a will is revocable by the testator any time prior to death. In this related sense it is said that a will is ambulatory in nature in that it has no effect until the death of the testator. Therefore, a will is merely a declaration of the testator's intentions until his death, and any potential beneficiary under the will runs the risk that the testator will dispose of his property inter vivos — he may dispose of the subject matter of the gift in the will

before it takes effect. Moreover, there is also the risk that on the testator's death his liabilities and debts will exceed the value of his assets, and the property, which is left to the beneficiary, might have to be sold to pay these debts.

4. The above management of the deceased's estate is carried out by the *personal representatives* of the testator, who are usually appointed under the will as *executors* of the estate. In the absence of an appointment by will, the personal representatives are appointed by the court, when they would be known as *administrators*. These representatives administer the affairs of the estate, pay off the debts, funeral expenses, etc., and then distribute the property as directed by the will. To exercise their appropriate functions, the executors apply to the court for a grant of probate, while the administrators are given a grant of letters of administration.

The second type of succession is labelled *intestate succession*. In this instance there is no will, or the will made is invalid, or ineffective, or it does not dispose of all of the deceased's property. The last scenario is termed a *partial intestacy*. Unlike testate succession where the deceased has quite a significant amount of freedom to distribute his property, in an intestate situation the property is distributed automatically in accordance with the rules of intestacy laid out by the Succession Act 1965.

Testate succession

The primary concern here will be with the making of wills, that is, the technical formalities required as a first step in the drafting of a will. There will also be a brief discussion on the *construction* of a will — how the courts go about interpreting the intention of the testator — and there will be an examination of the limits on the freedom of the testator to dispose of his property.

The making of wills

A will can be defined as a formal document that sets out how the testator wishes to dispose of his property on death. A person may make as many wills as he wishes, though usually the only relevant one is the last valid will made before his death, as this normally revokes prior wills. The following are considered as the basic necessities of the contents of a will:

- the testator's name and address
- a revocation clause
- a clause appointing at least one (but preferably two or more) executors
- a list of legacies (gifts of money or goods)
- a list of devises (gifts of real property)
- a residuary clause, disposing of the remainder of the estate
- the date
- the testator's signature
- the attestation clause or *testimonium*.

The capacity to make a will

For a will to be valid in Ireland, the testator must be aged 18 or over (or be, or have been, married). He must act of his own free will and must be of sound mind, memory and understanding. These conditions are laid down by Section 77(1) of the Succession Act 1965 and, in practice, the above requirements mean that the testator must understand that he is making a will; he must know the nature and extent of his property and he must be able to recall the people who might be expected to benefit from his estate.

The capacity to make a will may be proved by affidavit evidence or oral testimony from a doctor or solicitor who attended the deceased at the time the will was made. In the last resort, the courts will decide whether a testator had testamentary capacity, that is, whether the will in question was the will of a free and capable testator. Traditionally, the courts have given a fairly liberal meaning to mental capacity in an effort to uphold and protect the freedom of the testator; see further *Banks v Goodfellow* (1870) LR 5 QB 549.

The formalities of making a will

The basic formalities are fourfold, in that the will must be in writing; the document must be signed at the end by the testator (or by someone in his presence and by his direction); the signature must be written or acknowledged in the presence of two witnesses, both present at the same time and the witnesses must sign in the presence of the testator, but not necessarily in each other's presence.

These formalities of writing, signature and attestation are contained in Section 78 of the Succession Act, which incorporated many of the provisions of Section 9 of the Wills Act 1837. In practice, although Section 78 of the Succession Act does not require it, it is important that a standard form of attestation be used. The use of such a clause gives rise to the presumption *omnia praesumuntur rite esse acta* — everything is presumed to have been properly executed. The *testimonium* or attestation clause shows that the provisions of the Succession Act 1965 have been complied with. Its absence will not invalidate the will, but the Probate Office will require an affidavit from a subscribing witness.

The typical attestation clause might read:

> Signed by the testator as and for his last will and testament in the presence of us, both present at the same time, and signed by us in his presence.

The witnesses normally sign under this clause, but the will is not invalidated if they sign elsewhere. Similarly, an undated will is not necessarily invalid, but a witness will have to swear that the will was executed before the testator died.

The above points about the possible need of the witnesses to submit affidavit evidence to the court in certain situations raises the question as regards the competency of the witnesses. There are generally no special requirements as to the competence of the witnesses in terms of age or intelligence, etc. Indeed, Section 81 of the Succession Act states:

> If a person who attests the execution of a will, is, at the time of execution or at any time afterwards, incompetent to be admitted a witness to prove the execution the will shall not on that account be invalid.

However, under Section 82 of the Succession Act a witness or his spouse cannot generally benefit under a will. There is nothing however to stop a creditor from being a witness (Section 83 — the debt will not be affected); but a clause in the will agreeing a fee for drawing up or executing the will will be void if the solicitor or a member of his firm (or their spouses) act as a witness.

Alterations in a will

Any obliteration, insertion or alteration in a will after its execution is invalid unless the testator and witnesses sign near the alteration or unless the changes are proved to have been in the will before its execution. In short, unattested alterations made to the will are presumed at law to have been made after the execution of the will itself and therefore will not be upheld at a court of law. Thus, it is clearly desirable that in order to validate such alterations that the testator and witnesses should sign or initial the alterations wherever they are made as per Section 86 of the Succession Act. Section 86 facilitates this prudent practice by permitting alterations to be duly executed by the placing of the signatures of the testator and the witnesses in the margin or near to the alterations, or at the foot or end of, or opposite to, a memorandum referring to such alterations that are written on some other part of the will.

The revocation of a will

As a general rule a will remains revocable — changeable — until the death of the testator. A will can be revoked in a number of ways.

First, under Section 85(2) of the Succession Act, a properly executed later will or codicil, which expressly revokes all earlier testamentary dispositions, is the usual practice if a testator changes his mind about the content of his will. The testator makes a new will and inserts in the new will a clause expressly revoking all prior wills; for example:

I hereby revoke all testamentary dispositions heretofore made by me.

The revocation clause must revoke codicils and other testamentary dispositions, as well as former wills.

Second, Section 85(2) provides that it is not necessary to make a new will to revoke the old one. A will can also be revoked in whole or in part by some writing declaring an intention to revoke it and executed in the manner in which a will is required to be executed. Section 85(2) of the Succession Act also provides that a will can be revoked by burning, tearing or otherwise destroying the will.

Finally, under Section 85(1) of the Succession Act a will is automatically revoked by the subsequent marriage of the testator. This seems to be a policy decision having regard to the position of the new spouse. However, where the will is made in contemplation of marriage it is not revoked by that marriage.

The construction of a will

In the construction of a will the primary objective of the court is to determine the intention of the testator. It could be said that in this instance the courts take a schematic approach — in interpreting the testator's intention the courts take contextual account of the will as a whole. Words used by the testator will be given their natural and ordinary meaning unless this would lead to inconsistencies or absurdities. Similarly, where a testator uses words which have a generally recognised technical or legal meaning, the assumption is made that he intended that technical meaning; see further *Thorn v Dickens* [1906] WN 54 where the will stated 'All to mother'. The court accepted that the testator had always referred to his wife as 'mother'.

The courts are anxious to do whatever they can to uphold the freedom of the testator and traditionally they have not intervened even if the provision appeared mean, capricious or eccentric, for example, even if the will was made in cruel indifference to deserving immediate family members. Indeed, the courts often tried to put themselves in the place of the testator in an attempt to determine his intention. This largely subjective approach is known as the *armchair principle*.

Despite the fact that the courts were armed with general rules of interpretation and the armchair principle, it must be admitted that they have adopted a quite restrictive approach in that they held that the statutory requirement of writing made the will itself the primary and sole evidence of the testator's intention. As it was put euphemistically, the court was confined in its interpretation to the 'four corners of the will'. This meant that while extrinsic evidence was admissible to clarify what the testator had written, for example, if any external documents are mentioned in the will they should be produced, it was not admissible to help determine what the testator intended to write; see further *In re Julian* [1950] IR 57.

Some modification of the existing law was attempted in the Succession Act 1965 and Section 90 of the Act provides:

> Extrinsic evidence shall be admissible to show the intention of the testator, and to assist in the construction of, or to explain any contradiction in, a will.

Moreover, Section 99 of the Act states:

> If the purport of a devise or bequest admits more than one interpretation, then, in case of doubt, the interpretation according to which devise or bequest will be operative shall be preferred.

In *Rowe v Law* [1978] IR 501, the Supreme Court considered that admission of extrinsic evidence in this context could subvert the formal requirements for the execution of wills as set out in Section 78 of the same Act; see further *O'Connell v Bank of Ireland* [1998] 2 IR 596.

It is suggested that the standard for admitting extrinsic evidence under Section 90 of the Succession Act should be that if the terms of the will are not clarified properly and there is a danger that the estate will lapse into intestacy and be deemed inoperative, as per Section 99 of the Succession Act, extrinsic evidence should be deemed admissible; see further *Re Curtin* [1991] 2 IR 562 and *Mulhern v Brennan* [1999] 3 IR 528. In *Mulhern*, McCracken, J., cited Esher, M.R., in *Re Harrison* (1885) 30 Ch. D. 390, p. 393:

> There is one rule of construction, which is to my mind a golden rule: that when a testator has executed a will in solemn form you must assume that he did not intend to make it a solemn farce; that he did not

intend to die intestate when he has gone through the form of making a will. You ought, if possible, to read the will so as to lead to a testacy, not an intestacy.

Freedom of testation

Freedom of testation is a common law concept. Other legal systems, particularly the civilian systems of continental Europe (and indeed the old Brehon laws), placed limits on the testator's freedom by providing a fixed share of a deceased's estate for his surviving spouse and children. The Irish legislature was impressed by the greater equity of the civilian systems and sought to replicate many of those provisions in Parts IX and X of the Succession Act.

Under Section 111 of the Act the surviving spouse may receive a fixed share of the deceased's estate, while under Section 117 the surviving children have a right to apply to the court for provision to be made out of the deceased's estate on the grounds that the testator has failed to make proper provision for the applicant children in accordance with his means.

The rights of the surviving spouse and those of the children will be discussed separately. All proceedings relating to these parts of the Succession Act are heard in private as per Sections 119 and 122 of the Act.

Legal right of the surviving spouse

The right of a surviving spouse to a share in the testator's estate is contained in Section 111 of the Succession Act, 1965. Section 111 provides that if the testator leaves a spouse and no children, the spouse shall have a right to one-half of the estate. If the testator leaves a spouse and issue, the spouse is then entitled to one-third of the estate; see further *O'Dwyer v Keegan* [1997] 2 IR 585 on the automatic nature of this right.

Section 112 of the Act goes on to provide that if the will does not make provision for the spouse, the spouse obtains this legal share in the estate in priority to any devises, bequests or shares contained in the will. Accordingly, if a testator draws up his will and in it leaves a devise or bequest to a spouse in a will; can the surviving spouse claim both? No. Under Section 115(1)(a) the surviving spouse must elect to take either that devise or bequest or the share to which she is entitled. If the spouse does not elect, then the spouse is automatically taken to have chosen that which is given to her under the will. This presumption against the legal right share is contained in Section 115(1)(b). However, if the spouse does elect to take the legal right share, the spouse may further elect, as per Section 115(3) to take any bequest or devise to her under the will which is less in value than the legal right share, in partial satisfaction thereof.

As per Section 115(4), it is the duty of the personal representatives to notify the spouse in writing of the above right of election. This right must be exercised by the surviving spouse within the six months from receipt by the spouse of such notification or one year from the first taking out of representation of the deceased's estate, whichever is the later.

It must be noted that in the above instances we have presumed that the testator died wholly testate, with all his estate distributed and dealt with in the will. However, this is not always the case and the testator might die partially intestate, that is, not all of the deceased's property is distributed by the will. In such a scenario the surviving spouse may elect, under Section 115(2)(a), to take *either* the legal right share *or* their share under intestacy together with any devise or bequest under the will of the deceased. In default of election, the surviving spouse is presumed, under Section 115(2)(b), to take the share under the intestacy, together with any devise or bequest under the will and shall not be entitled to take any share as a legal right.

Two final points need to be made on the legal right of the surviving spouse, before some examples are given. First, as per Section 113 of the Succession Act, the legal right of a spouse may be renounced in an ante-nuptial contract made in writing between the parties to an intended marriage. The legal right of the surviving spouse may also be renounced in writing by the spouse after marriage and during the lifetime of the testator.

The final point that needs to be made is that under Section 56 of the Succession Act the surviving spouse also has the right to require that the family dwelling (Section 56(1)) and household chattels (Section 56(2)) be appropriated. This right arises whether the deceased dies testate or intestate. This means that where the estate of a deceased person includes a dwelling in which, at the time of the deceased's death, the surviving spouse was ordinarily resident, the surviving spouse may require that the personal representatives, in writing, appropriate the dwelling in, or towards satisfaction of, her legal share.

Section 56(14) states that the term 'dwelling' includes any garden or portion of ground attached to and usually occupied with the dwelling or otherwise required for the amenity or convenience of the dwelling; see further *Re Hamilton, Hamilton v Armstrong* [1984] ILRM 306. Section 56(14) also defines the term 'household chattels'. It is to include furniture, linen, china, glass, books and other chattels of ordinary household use or ornament and also consumable stores, garden effects and domestic animals. It does not include any chattels used at the death of the deceased for business or professional purposes or money or security for money.

Under Section 56(4) it is the duty of the personal representatives to notify the surviving spouse in writing of this right of appropriation. And Section 56(5)(a) states that the right of appropriation cannot be exercised after the expiration of six months from the receipt by the surviving spouse of such notification or one year from the first taking out of representation of the deceased's estate, whichever is the later.

If the share of the surviving spouse is insufficient to enable an appropriation to be made, Section 56(3) permits the right to appropriate to be exercised by the surviving spouse in relation to the share of any infant for whom the surviving spouse is a trustee. If the dwelling house and chattels are worth more than the shares of the surviving spouse and any such child, the surviving spouse may settle up the balance by payment of money as per Section 56(9). The court has discretion under the Section 56(10) to waive the payment of this balance or at least reasonably limit the payment of it in special circumstances of hardship.

It must also be noted that there are limits on the right to demand appropriation and with respect to certain types of dwelling the right to require appropriation is subject to the authorisation of the court. Section 56(5)(b) notes that the court must be satisfied that the exercise of the right of appropriation is unlikely to diminish the value of the assets of the deceased other than the dwelling or to make it more difficult to dispose of them. This is particularly true where the dwelling forms part of a building and the estate is the whole building or even more divisively where the dwelling is held as part of an estate of agricultural land.

The difficulty is summed up simply: *the statute provides for appropriation*; but how will this affect the value and viable usage of the estate? For example, a husband and wife, who have no children, live on a farm. The husband dies and it is revealed that his will has properly and fully disposed of the farm to a nephew. The surviving spouse exercises her right to appropriate the dwelling house in which she is ordinarily resident. The difficulty for the nephew is how to run the farm without being in control of the main farmhouse and place of residence; see further *H v H* [1978] IR 138, where the Supreme Court held that the onus was on the surviving spouse to demonstrate that the appropriation would not diminish the value of the property as a whole and that this onus had not been discharged.

Example: Section 111 of the Succession Act

In his will the recently deceased Mr Ryan left his wedding ring, worth €1,000, to his wife, Mary. The will also left a legacy of €31,000 in favour of Mr Ryan's brother, Paddy, a legacy of €18,000 in favour of his sister, Betty, and a legacy of €10,000 to a neighbour. All debts being paid, Mr Ryan's estate is valued at €114,000. Mr Ryan and his wife had two children, Neil and Eoin, but the will made no reference to them.

Discuss Mary's rights in this situation.

The total value of Mr Ryan's estate is €114,000. €60,000 of Mr Ryan's estate is disposed of by the will — €1,000 (ring) plus €31,000 (legacy to Paddy) plus €18,000 (legacy to Betty) plus €10,000 (legacy to neighbour). €54,000 is undistributed. Thus, Mr Ryan has died partially intestate. In such a scenario the surviving spouse (Mary) may elect, under Section 115(2)(a), to take *either* the legal right share *or* her share under intestacy, together with any devise or bequest under the will of the deceased. In default of election the surviving spouse is presumed, under Section 115(2)(b), to take the share under the intestacy, together with any devise or bequest under the will and shall not be entitled to take any share as a legal right.

As per Section 115(4), it is the duty of the personal representatives to notify the spouse in writing of the above right of election. This right must be exercised by the surviving spouse within the six months from receipt by the spouse of such notification or one year from the first taking out of representation of the deceased's estate, whichever is the later. In applying Section 115(2)(a) to the above scenario if Mary decides to elect, she will face the following choice.

1. She can elect to take her legal right share under Section 111, which, given there are children, is one-third of the total estate — one-third of €114,000, equals €38,000.

or

2. She can take her share under intestacy together with any devise or bequest under the will of the deceased:

    *   *Share under intestacy* — there are children, therefore as per the rules of intestacy (see below), Mary receives two-thirds of that which has not been disposed of, that is, two-thirds of €54,000, equals €36,000.
    *   *Will* — Under the will Mary received a wedding ring worth €1,000.

    Total: €36,000 (share on intestacy) + €1,000 (under the will) = €37,000.

Under Section 115(2)(a), if Mrs X does elect she will presumably choose her legal share (of £€8,000), though it must be noted that in default of election the surviving spouse is presumed, under Section 115(2)(b), to take the share under the intestacy, together with any devise or bequest under the will (in our example, this amounts to €37,000) and shall not be entitled to take any share as a legal right. As per Section 115(4), it is the duty of the personal representatives to notify the spouse in writing of the above right of election.

The position of Neil and Eoin in this example highlights the next issue.

Legal rights of the surviving children

Unlike the rights of the surviving spouse, which is a fixed legal share, the rights of the surviving child are dependent on the judicial discretion of the courts. Section 117(1) of the Succession Act states that:

> Where, on application by or on behalf of a child of the testator, the court is of the opinion that the testator has failed in his moral duty to make proper provision for the child in accordance with his means, by will or otherwise, the court may order that such provision shall be made for the child out of the estate as the court thinks just.

Section 117(2) goes on to state that the court should consider the application from the point of view of the prudent and just parent taking into account the position and circumstance of each child.

The definition of the term 'child', as per Section 3 of the Status of Children Act 1987 includes children born out of wedlock — *non-marital children*. Section 117 was specifically amended in this regard by Section 31 of the 1987 Act.

Before we examine the extent to which the courts have interpreted these legislative provisions it must be noted that the final subsection to Section 117, subsection 3, reminds us that an order making provision for an applicant child cannot affect the legal right of a surviving spouse or any devise or bequest to the spouse to which he or she is entitled to on intestacy. This last provision highlights the fact that in practice once the expenses of the estate have been paid off and the surviving spouse has been taken care of there may be very little left for the children to apply for in any event.

Overall, the position of the surviving spouse is much more privileged in the legislation than the children. While the spouse may automatically receive his or her legal right share, the children must apply to gain the assistance of Section 117. Under Section 117(6), as amended by Section 46 of the Family Law Divorce Act 1996, the children have only six months from the taking out of representation of the deceased's estate to apply to the court. In addition, unlike Section 111 where the personal representatives are under an obligation to inform the surviving spouse of her rights, under a Section 117 application, the personal representatives of the deceased's estate are under no obligation to inform the children of their rights.

Section 117

The scope and effect of Section 117 was first considered in *In the Goods of GM*:

FM v TAM (1972) 106 ILTR 82. Briefly, the facts of the case were that the testator was a substantial property owner both in Ireland and in England. He left all his property in Ireland on trust for his wife for life and on her death to two nephews. There were no children of the marriage but the couple had, somewhat to the testator's annoyance, adopted a child. Section 110 of the Succession Act provides that an adopted child is to be seen in the same light as a child born of the marriage. The testator made no provision in the will for this adopted child and the child made an application to the court under Section 117.

At the time of the application the plaintiff was 32 years old, a merchant seaman, married with two children of his own. Among the arguments put forward by the husband's estate was that the child was in no way dependent on the testator at the time of the testator's death. Kenny, J., rejected this argument and went on to give a general review of the principles a court should take into account in hearing — in camera — a Section 117 application.

First, as regards the independent child argument, Kenny, J., pointed out that while it was the case in England and some Commonwealth countries that their equivalent legislation is limited to those children who are dependent on the testator, this was not the case under Section 117 of the Succession Act, which makes no mention of such a requirement. However, that is not to say that the duty of the testator to his children under Section 117 is absolute in that the testator must always leave something in his will for the child. The legislation clearly states that proper provision may be made by 'will or otherwise'. Therefore it may be that during his lifetime the testator made provision for the child through gifts or settlements, for example, he may have paid for an education, and this would in the circumstances be sufficient to discharge the duty of care under Section 117.

In this, it is obvious that the courts will regard the duty of the testator from an objective point of view — the reasonable outsider — and that it is irrelevant whether or not the testator subjectively regarded himself as having made proper provision for his children. It follows that it may arise that a testator will do his best to discharge his duty and thus be blameless but he may still as a practical matter have failed to make proper provision for his issue. Later case law will demonstrate this objectivity in practice.

A second point made by Kenny, J., was that it is the date of death that is the relevant time in assessing the question of failure in a moral duty by a testator. It would be no answer to an application to demonstrate that at the time it was made a particular will made proper provision for the applicant. Why? In short, circumstances might well have changed after the making of the will and, as Kenny, J., quite rightly stated, the duty created by Section 117 extends to modifying the provisions of the will to ensure that they remain satisfactory.

Thirdly, Kenny, J., remarked that not only must the existence of a moral duty to make proper provision for a child be judged objectively and at the date of the testator's death, it may also depend on the following five criteria:

- the amount left to the surviving spouse or the value of the legal right of the spouse to which she is entitled if she so elects
- the number of the testator's children, their ages and their positions in life at the time of the testator's death
- the means of the testator
- the age of the child whose case is being considered and his or her financial position and prospects in life
- whether the testator has already in his lifetime made proper provision for the child.

Applying the above principles to the instant case Kenny, J., held that, given the means of the testator, he had failed to make proper provision for his child and in the circumstances a prudent and just parent would, in the court's opinion, have given the son one-half of his estate.

In sum, and taking the lead from Mr Justice Kenny's seminal judgement, the subsequent case law regarding Section 117 can be examined under three headings. First, the objective manner in which the courts view the testator's duty. Second, that it is the time of death not the time of execution of the will that is the proper time to assess the failure in duty and, finally, that the quality of the personal relationship between the testator and the child may have had a critical effect on the child's application.

Objectivity

Even if the testator genuinely thinks that proper provision has been made by him for his offspring in his will, the court may, on an objective review of the provisions of the will, deem otherwise. This often occurs where the testator feels that as the child is being adequately provided for from another source there is little need for him to make testamentary provision for that child.

It was not uncommon for testators, particularly testators in rural Ireland, to misconceive the extent of their moral duty to make proper provision for their daughters and more particularly their married daughters. However, in *Re NSM* (1973) 107 ILTR 1, Kenny, J., reminded the court that married women were not a distinct class for the purposes of Section 117. While the fact that a daughter is married and well provided for by other funds must be taken into account by the court, this does not relieve the testator *in toto* of his moral duty to provide for his daughters in accordance with his means.

The fact that the applicant child is provided for from other sources cannot be a bar on the testator's moral duty is also shown in the case of *Re Michael Looney*, 2 November 1970, High Court, Kenny, J. In that case, Kenny, J., observed that the statutory obligation of a county council to maintain a child with learning disabilities in an institution did not relieve her father of his moral obligation to provide for her in accordance with his means.

Time of assessment

According to Mr Justice Kenny in *In the Goods of GM* it is the death of the testator that is the crucial time in determining whether the testator has properly provided for the applicant child; see further *Re W: WvD*, 28 May 1975, High Court, Parke, J.

It seems from the case *Re NSM* (1973) 107 ILTR 1 that it is appropriate to take into account events after the death of the testator, which should have been reasonably foreseeable to the testator in his lifetime. In the instant case, the testator had given the residue of his large estate to his youngest son. As a result of prolonged and expensive litigation that followed the death of the testator, the value of the residuary gift had shrunk considerably. Mr Justice Kelly stated that it should have been reasonable for the testator to foresee the legal dispute that arose after his death and the adverse affect it would have on that which was given to the youngest son.

Furthermore, in *MPD v MD* [1981] ILRM 179 Carroll, J., stated that where, at the date of death, the court established that there was a failure in moral duty by the testator in devising an order to make proper provision for the children, the court could even take into account the situation at the time of the actual hearing of the Section 117 application. To this end, the court would be able to take into account events unforeseeable at the time of the testator's death such as a serious car accident, an illness or conversely winning the lottery. Moreover, if the event after the will was sufficiently serious as to transform the whole environment to which the will had been geared, the above approach would in effect give the court the power to make provision out of the estate to suit the present situation and, depending on the circumstances, this may be only right and proper.

In the present case, Carroll, J., remarked that this approach would have permitted her, in making provision for the applicant, to take into account the fact that the testator's assets had doubled in value since the date of death. On the facts of the case, Carroll, J., held that she was precluded from making an order by the fact that the relevant application was made outside the one-year time limit laid down by subsection 6 of Section 117 (now amended to six months.)

In summary, therefore, it seems from the case law that under Section 117 the testator in making his will is under an obligation to take into account events foreseeable at the time of his death and the courts, in considering the will, have the power to make provision even for events unforeseeable at the time of the testator's death where they consider that at his death the testator has failed in his moral duty to properly provide for the applicant child.

Relationship with the testator

In the course of his judgement in *In the Goods of GM*, Kenny, J., laid down five helpful criteria (see page 105) in considering a Section 117 application. Two of the five criteria noted that the courts, in considering a Section 117 application, should take into account the number of the testator's children, their ages and their positions in life at the time of the testator's death and, where appropriate, the age of the child whose case is being considered and his or her financial position and prospects in life.

The Supreme Court affirmed these guidelines in *C and Ch v WC and TC* [1990] 2 IR 143. However, Finlay, C.J., reminded the Court that in a Section 117 application the onus of proof lay firmly on the applicant child to demonstrate that there was a 'positive failure' in the testator's moral duty. A discussion of the term 'positive failure' can be found in *EB v SS* [1998] 4 IR 527. In this case, the applicant son made a Section 117 application in regard to his deceased mother's estate. The testatrix had four children and prior to her death in 1992 she had made substantial provisions for each child to the tune of £275,000. Under the terms of her will, she left a number of monies to her grandchildren and the residue to named charities. There was no provision in her will for her children, as she believed that she had made adequate provision for them during her life time.

It seems that at the time of making her will the deceased knew that the applicant had squandered his advancement. By the time of the testatrix's death all the monies were spent. He was unemployed, separated and had three young dependant children in his care. Overall, the applicant had a fraught personal history. His father had employed him in the family business and put him through college. His father had also purchased a house for him with one of his sisters jointly. However, in the mid-1980s the applicant developed serious alcohol and drug problems, though the court accepted that shortly after his mother's death he was 'reformed'.

At the time of trial he was in receipt of social welfare; he had no savings and his only asset was his share in the house. He instituted Section 117 proceedings. While he acknowledged that provision had already been made for him during the testatrix's lifetime, he argued that his application should be considered in the light of the circumstances existing at the date of his mother's death and he reminded the court that his mother was at all times well aware of his personal circumstances.

In the High Court the application was rejected, Lavan, J., felt that there was no positive failure of the part of the testatrix, the majority in the Supreme Court felt likewise. The applicant had received enough provision and he was to get no more. Barron, J., dissented and he argued that the applicant had genuine needs and that provision could and should be made for these needs. Barron, J., further noted that the actual intention of the applicant was to provide for his children, that is, the grandchildren, thus, Barron, J., suggested that a supervised trust, only to be used for the needs of the applicant's children, should be set up.

Keane, J., (as he then was) for the majority rejected the notion of a trust. Considerable financial assistance had already been provided for the applicant and further provision for him might well be squandered again, even if provided for under the terms of the trust. In any event, Keane, J., noted Section 117 referred to the deceased's children only, nothing could be done under Section 117 (in the form of a trust or otherwise) to extend the Section 117 protection to grandchildren. If Section 117 were to be extended to these persons it would be up to the legislature to amend Section 117 to do so and was not the role of the courts.

Another recent Section 117 case of importance in this regard is *McDonald v Norris* [1999] 4 IR 301. In 1963 the testator was badly injured and shortly after that the plaintiff, then aged 14, left school to run the estate with the help of his mother. The mother died in 1968 and gradually the plaintiff ran the estate as a whole. The estate was quite large; approximately 400 acres of farmland, and the applicant effectively had the run of the place with his father maintaining an account for him at a local shop. A younger brother also existed though he showed little interest in the farm.

In the early 1980s the testator moved in with the Norris family. On the testator's death in 1993 most of the farm was left to a younger member of the Norris family. In retrospect, it must have become clear to the applicant that his title to the farm was not secure as it was not signed over as of yet, and more than likely he felt threatened by the Norris connection. Furthermore, the plaintiff got married in 1981 and the testator took a dislike to the wife and refused to attend the marriage. Ultimately a row developed to the extent that the testator sought an injunction to remove the applicant from the land. The applicant ignored the court order and eventually in the mid-1980s he was thrown in jail for 11 months for contempt.

While in prison, the applicant's wife continued to run the farm but the testator transferred some lands to the younger brother and also some lands to the Norris family. These *inter vivos* transactions were carried out at undervalue with the clear intention of circumventing the applicant's claims.

On release from prison the applicant was clearly embittered. He returned to live with his wife on the remaining part of the original estate. Locally, he organised a campaign of terror and intimidation against his ailing father and also the Norris family.

The testator eventually died in the 1990s and under the terms of the will a member of the Norris family received the remainder of the original estate. The applicant, who received a paltry £5,000, made an application to the court under Section 117. He argued that he had left school at an early age to assist on the home farm, whereby the testator had a moral obligation to provide for him and in particular to allow him to remain on the lands.

The High Court adjudged the appalling nature of the child's behaviour towards the testator as to be of such an extent as to negate any Section 117 obligations. Moreover, the High Court argued that the applicant had for a long period the total and free run of the estate and that this could be seen as an advancement. The Supreme Court reversed the decision; they rejected the advancement argument as a temporary provision only. The Supreme Court acknowledged that the applicant's behaviour was appalling but the Court felt that Section 117 is primarily concerned with the obligations of the testator to provide for the child. The Supreme Court noted that the testator had a role to play in the hostile relationship; for example, he had attempted to eject the son from the land. The Supreme Court noted that account must be taken that underlying the testator's intentions at all times since the early 1980s was his concern to provide for non-family members. The applicant child should be allowed to remain and inherit the remaining 170 acres of the estate.

In sum, the Supreme Court was of the opinion that at first instance the outright hostility of a child towards a parent will understandably diminish the moral obligations of the parent to provide for that child, but that the courts must be aware that the hostility may in fact also have been contributed to and prompted by the actions of the parent.

In reading this informative case students will also see reference to Section 121 of the Succession Act, which states that any disposition made by the testator outside his will and within three years of the testator's death that the court thinks was made with the intention of disinheriting the child will be treated as if part of the will. Moreover, in *McDonald v Norris* [1999] 4 IR 301 reference is made to Section 120 of the Succession Act, which identifies persons who are deemed unworthy to succeed to the estate of the deceased person. For example, under Section 120(4) an applicant who has committed an offence against the deceased, the spouse of the deceased or any other child of the deceased, which is punishable by more than two years in prison, is absolutely barred to a claim under Section 117. And as per Section 120(5) any share, which a person is precluded from taking under Section 120, will be distributed as if that person had predeceased the testator.

The courts have extensively construed the scheme of Section 117 of the Succession Act. In a Section 117 application, the courts can take into consideration a range of factors including the relationship between the parties, the financial and social position of the applicant, even events which the testator could not have foreseen occurring after his death but which at the time of the hearing may have quite a considerable effect on the terms of the will.

Intestate succession

A person dies intestate when (a) he has failed to make a will disposing of his property on death or (b) he has made a will that has not been properly executed or (c) the will is ineffective due, for example, to the fact that the sole beneficiary may have predeceased the testator. Furthermore, where the testator has not disposed of his entire property, a partial intestacy may ensue.

Basic rules

The rules governing intestate succession are contained in Part VI of the Succession Act. Part VI abolishes all the old and complicated rules of intestacy. These old rules now apply only to dispositions made before 1 January 1967, the day the Succession Act came into effect. The rules contained in Part VI are as follows.

Where an intestate dies leaving a spouse and no children (children are sometimes referred to as 'issue'), the spouse is entitled to the whole estate. If a spouse and children survive the intestate, the spouse takes two-thirds of the estate and the remainder is distributed among the issue. If an intestate dies leaving children and no spouse the entire estate is divided among the children. The division is *per stirpes* with the doctrine of representation applying: the issue of a child who predeceased the intestate will 'step into the shoes' of their dead parent and take the share he would have received, had he lived. For example:

X had four children, two sons and two daughters. X died intestate and was predeceased by two of his children D1 and S2. D1 had two children; S2 was

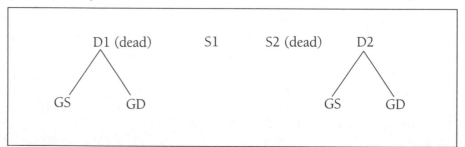

unmarried and had none. Each of X's children who is alive or represented by issue at X's death, form a 'stock of descent'. In the diagram there are three of these stocks — D1, S1 and D2. The intestate's estate will therefore be divided into three parts. The children of D1 will share their mother's one-third interest, each taking one-sixth of the deceased's estate; but the children of D2 will get nothing as their mother is still alive and entitled to her one-third share.

Where neither spouse nor children survive the intestacy, but both parents of the intestate survive, then the estate will be distributed equally among the parents. If only one parent survives the intestate, that parent will take the whole estate. If an intestate dies leaving neither spouse nor issue nor parent, the estate will be distributed among the intestate's brothers and sisters equally, the doctrine of representation applying. If there are no surviving brothers and sisters, the estate will be divided equally among the surviving nieces and nephews. The doctrine of representation does not apply from this point onwards. If there are no surviving nephews or nieces, the estate goes to the 'next of kin', as defined by Section 71(2) of the Succession Act:

> Degrees of blood relationship of a direct lineal ancestor shall be computed by counting upwards from the intestate to that ancestor, and degrees of blood relationship of any other relative shall be ascertained by counting upwards from the intestate to the nearest ancestor common to the intestate and the relative, and then downwards from that ancestor to the relative; but, where a direct lineal ancestor and any other relative are so ascertained to be within the same degree of blood relationship to the intestate, the other relative shall be preferred to the exclusion of the direct lineal ancestor.

In calculating the next of kin under the above provision it is best to keep in mind the following three points:

1. To locate an ancestor, count upwards from the intestate to the ancestor, for example, father 1, grandfather 2, great grandfather 3, etc.

2. To locate a relative, count upwards from the intestate to the ancestor common to both the intestate and the relative and then down to the relative, for example, for an uncle the common relative is the grandfather, which is two steps up, and then count back down to the uncle, which is one step, giving a total of three steps.

3. If the ancestor and relative are of the same degree, then the estate, as a matter of policy, is awarded to the relative on the grounds that it is

presumed that the relative will live longer than the ancestor.

Example A

A deceased dies intestate and is survived by a first cousin and a grand uncle. Explain how it is determined who will get the property.

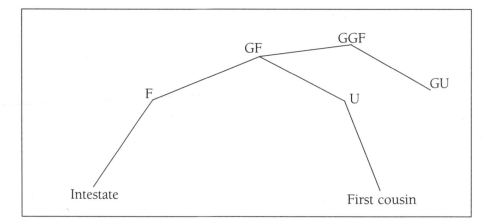

Grand uncle: Count up to the direct lineal ancestor common to both the grand uncle and the intestate, which is the great grandfather. This accounts for three steps. Then count down from the great grandfather to the grand uncle. This is one step, which implies a total of four steps.

First cousin: Count up to a direct lineal ancestor common to both the first cousin and the intestate, which is the grandfather. This accounts for two steps. Then count down from the grandfather to the first cousin. This accounts for two steps, which implies a total of four steps.

As a result, both the grand uncle and the first cousin are equally entitled to the estate.

Example B

Mary dies intestate survived by her brother-in-law, James, her uncle, Henry, and her grand niece, Debbie. Discuss the distribution of Mary's estate.

Brother-in-law: A brother-in-law is not a blood relative under Section 71(2) of the Act.

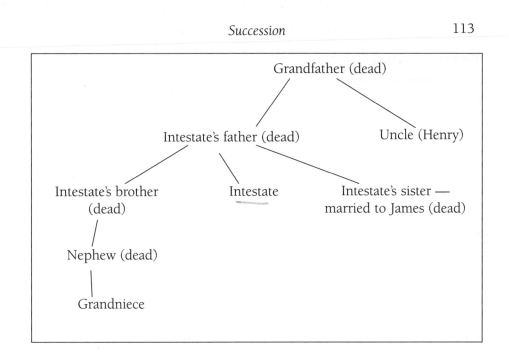

Uncle: Count up to ancestor common to both the uncle and the intestate, which is the grandfather. This accounts for two steps. Then count down from the grandfather to the uncle. This is one step, which implies a total of three steps.

Grandniece: Count up to a direct lineal ancestor common to both the grandniece and the intestate, which is the intestate's father. This accounts for one step. Then count down from the intestate's father to the grandniece. This accounts for three steps, which implies a total of four steps.

According to the rules of intestacy as per Section 71(2) of the Succession Act, Mary's uncle will receive the estate, as he is the deemed the next of kin.

Finally, if a next of kin cannot be ascertained it is held that the State shall take the estate as the ultimate intestate successor, as per Section 73(1). The Minister for Finance may waive this right of claim under Section 73(2) of the Act. It is unusual for the Minster to waive the State's right of claim, although he may do so where there is evidence that the deceased may have intended a charity to benefit or that some person not blood-related to the deceased has a considerable moral claim to a share in the deceased's estate, for example, a loyal housekeeper.

Further reading

Brady, J., *Succession Law in Ireland* 2nd edn. Dublin: Butterworths, 1995.

Coughlan, P., *Property Law*, 2nd edn. Dublin: Gill & MacMillan, 1998, Chapter 18.

Keating, A., *Probate Law and Practice*. Dublin: Round Hall Sweet & Maxwell, 1999.

Keating, A., *Probate Law and Practice Casebook*. Dublin: Round Hall Sweet & Maxwell, 1999.

Lyall, A., *Land Law in Ireland*, 2nd edn. Dublin: Round Hall Sweet & Maxwell, 2000, Chapter 26.

Wylie, J., *Irish Land Law*, 3rd edn. Dublin: Butterworths, 1997, Chapters 14 and 15.

Wylie, J., *Irish Landlord and Tenant Law* 2nd edn. Dublin: Butterworths, 1998.

Self-test

1. John Waldron died on 1 April 2000. Waldron's marriage to Sheila, which had been a tempestuous affair, produced no children. In his will, John left all his property, consisting of a 40-acre farm and dwelling house, in which he had resided with Sheila, to his nephew Cormac, for Cormac's benefit absolutely. Cormac was delighted, as although the holding is small, it is compact and productive. Moreover, it is extremely fertile, can be intensely farmed and comes with its own water and sewage facilities located within its borders. The dwelling house is strategically situated in the geographical centre of the property and an extended driveway leading to the dwelling house from the main road neatly partitions the property. However, Cormac's delight is qualified when the personal representatives of John's estate inform him that his benefit is subject to Sheila's express right under the will to the exclusive use of a bedroom in the dwelling. Furthermore, the personal representatives inform Cormac that Sheila, as the surviving spouse, has other legal entitlements but they are unsure whether she will exercise these options.

    What are the 'other legal entitlements' available to Sheila and to what extent, if any, will these entitlements compromise the benefit given to Cormac under the will?

    ### Key points

    Consider generally the rights of the surviving spouse as contained in

Section 111 of the Succession Act 1965 and refer to Section 56 of the Succession Act 1965 as interpreted in, for example, *Re Hamilton, Hamilton* v *Armstrong* [1984] ILRM 306 and *H* v *H* [1978] IR 138.

2. Thomas Ryan married his first wife in 1958 and they had two children, Andrew and Brian. His wife died soon after Brian was born and Thomas married Mary in 1968. Thomas and Mary had three children, Charles, Denis and Edward. Andrew died in 1994 leaving one son, George. In May 1998, Thomas transferred all his assets, except his farm to Mary. He died in March 2001, having left his farm to Denis and Edward in equal shares. Brian complains that he and George got nothing. Charles also complains and argues that the reason he received nothing from the will was as a result of a long-standing quarrel that he had had with his father. Brian suffered a bad accident some years ago and is disabled from work. George is still at school. Charles has a pensionable post in the Civil Service.

Advise Brian, George and Charles.

Key points

Consider generally the rights of surviving children as contained in Section 117 of the Succession Act 1965. Also, refer to appropriate issues raised by case law, for example, proof of positive failure as in *EB* v *SS* [1998] 4 IR 527 and *McDonald* v *Norris* [1999] 4 IR 301.

11
LANDLORD AND TENANT LAW

Modern Irish landlord and tenant law begins with the Landlord and Tenant Amendment (Ireland) Act 1860. This influential piece of legislation is more commonly known as 'Deasy's Act', after the then Attorney General of Ireland who steered the bill through Westminster. According to Section 3 of the Act, the relationship of landlord and tenant exists where one party, whether pursuant to an express or implied agreement, holds land for or under another in consideration of any rent. The landlord is known as the *lessor* and the tenant as the *lessee*. To constitute such a tenancy, the tenant must have exclusive possession of the land, that is, the right to exclude the owner from the premises for a fixed term in consideration of the rent.

Traditionally, it was thought that exclusive possession was the principal feature distinguishing a lease from other similar concepts such as a licence. Recent developments in this area of the law seem to question this reasoning. (We will return later in this chapter to the manner in which the courts now distinguish between leases and licences.)

Formalities in the creation of a lease

Section 2 of the Statute of Frauds (Ireland) 1695 states:

> No action shall be brought to charge any person upon any contract or sale of lands or any interest therein, unless the agreement or some memorandum or note thereof shall be in writing and signed by the person to be charged or some other person lawfully authorised.

Section 4 of Deasy's Act slightly modified these requirements:

> Every lease or contract with respect to lands whereby the relation of landlord and tenant is intended to be created for any freehold estate or interest, or for any definite period of time not being from year-to-year or any lesser period, shall be by deed executed, or note in writing signed by the landlord or his agent thereunto lawfully authorised in writing.

The modifications initiated by Section 4 of Deasy's Act are that leases for any time period less than on a year-to-year basis do not have to be in writing or be created by any formal document, that is, they can be oral in nature. Any other agreements of this type, which are for more than a year in length, must be written and signed by the landlord (or by his agent as duly authorised) and then sent to the tenant.

Tenancies or leases which are equal to or less than year-to-year can be broken down into two distinguishable categories:

- periodic tenancies
- terms certain.

Typical of periodic tenancies are tenancies that last from year-to-year, month-to-month or week-to-week. They do not have to be written agreements. For example, in *Landy v Power* [1962-3] Ir Jur Rep 45 a shop was let under an oral agreement for a weekly periodic tenancy. A question arose over its validity. It was argued that as the agreement was not in writing it could not be enforced but the court ruled that, as it was a periodic tenancy of less than year-to-year in length, it fell outside the statutory formalities required by Deasy's Act.

The same rules apply where there is a grant for a term certain or, as Section 4 puts it, for a 'definite period of time', which is less than from 'year-to-year'; see further *Crane v Naughten* [1912] 2 IR 318 where the term certain was six months.

The status of a lease granted for one year certain was answered by Lord Denning in *Bernays v Prosser* [1963] 2 QB 592, p. 598:

> A tenancy from year-to-year is not only a tenancy for one year certain. It is something more, because the tenant, unless a notice to quit has been given, has a right to stay on after the end of the year and so on from year-to-year.

Finally, even when the formalities of Section 4 of Deasy's Act have not been complied with, for example, a two-year lease made orally only, the agreement may be still be enforceable in equity through what is known as the *doctrine of part performance*; see further *Walsh v Lonsdale* (1882) 21 Ch D 9 and *McCausland v Murphy* (1881) 9 LR Ir 9. In the latter case the court upheld the lease, despite its informality, on the grounds that the tenant had spent money on the premises.

Classification of tenancies

Terms certain and periodic tenancies are the principal classifications of tenancies.

Terms certain

A term certain is a tenancy for a definite and fixed period of time. It is a popular type of tenancy and can last for any fixed period ranging from a week to anything up to 10,000 years; see further *Re Sergie* [1954] NI 1. The courts may strike down leases which they regard as not being certain enough as regards their duration; see further *Lace* v *Chandler* [1944] KB 368, where the lease was based on the 'duration of the War'.

Periodic tenancies

In periodic tenancies, for example, week-to-week, month-to-month and year-to-year tenancies, the only thing certain or fixed is the original minimum period — one week or one month, etc. A key point about the classic periodic tenancy is that there is no certainty as regards maximum duration because if neither party takes any action to determine (terminate) the tenancy, for example, by giving notice, the successive periods can continue indefinitely. This 'roll-on' provision was given statutory recognition in Section 5 of Deasy's Act.

The lease agreement

At its most basic a lease agreement must have four essential terms:

- the names of the relevant parties
- a clear and exact description of the property in question
- the length of the lease, clearly stated and including the exact date of commencement
- a note of the rent reserved.

Generally, these fundamental terms will be uncontroversial and the key rights and duties of the landlord and tenant will depend upon the supplementary covenants or conditions that are contained in the tenancy agreement. These express covenants in the lease agreement may be automatically modified, even declared void by common law or, more frequently, by statute.

Covenants

A glance at any modern lease, for example, a typical lease for letting a private house or flat, will demonstrate that the tenant tends to be bound by a great many more covenants than the landlord. In an general sense, the common law and the older statutes underwrote this inequality in favour of the landlord. There are of course many good reasons for this, including the fact that the landlord after all owns the property. However, in recent times legislation has attempted to in some way redress the balance. A prime example of this is the Housing (Registration of Rented Houses) Regulations 1996 (SI 1996/30), which require that from 1 May 1996 a landlord must register his interest with the local authority. Failure to do so is an offence under Section 34 of the Housing Act 1992 carrying a maximum fine of £1,000 plus £100 for every day thereafter. There are similar penalties for breach of recent rent book and housing standards regulations.

Returning to the terms of a typical lease agreement, it is not unusual for the lease or tenancy agreement to contain no express covenants or agreements directed against the landlord other than an express covenant to respect the tenant's 'quiet enjoyment' of the property. This concept means that the tenant, on proper and timely payment of rent, may not be disturbed by any acts of the landlord, or any other person for whom he is responsible, unless due notice is given. Moreover, under Section 41 of Deasy's Act, even where the agreement does not expressly provide the right to quiet enjoyment, the statute provides that the tenant is implicitly entitled to have it without interference from the landlord or any of his agents for the duration of the lease so long as he performs his obligations under the lease; see further *Bowes v Dublin Corporation* [1965] IR 476.

Apart from the obligation by the landlord to respect the tenant's quiet enjoyment of the property, it is the tenant who is bound by the majority of the obligations. Of primary concern to the landlord is that the tenant uses and maintains the property in a responsible manner in order to protect and preserve the landlord's investment. Therefore, covenants relating to maintenance and repairs are a standard feature of modern leases and in general the tenant will be liable for daily maintenance and repair while the landlord will be responsible for any major structural and external repairs.

Repairs

A typical lease to let a private house or flat will generally include 'repair and maintain' covenants directed against both the tenant and the landlord.

Landlord

The landlord's repair covenant generally refers to major structural repairs. It is usually accompanied by a related covenant giving the landlord, or his agent, the right to enter or view the premises, at reasonable notice, in order to carry out the repairs. This is the only limitation on the tenant's right to exclusive possession and the landlord is not otherwise entitled to enter the premises and come and go as he pleases. Indeed, if the landlord so enters the premises and begins to repair it, he opens himself to liability in tort for any negligence in so repairing the premises; see further *Bowes* v *Dublin Corporation* [1965] IR 476 and *McCauliffe* v *Moloney* [1971] IR 200.

In the absence of an express 'repair and maintain' covenant in the lease, there was no implied liability under the common law on the landlord to repair the premises for major structural defects; see *Cowan* v *Factor* [1948] IR 128. However, over the years the common law itself and, more particularly, statute have largely qualified this freedom. For example, in the case of the letting of a *furnished* house it seems that the common law implicitly requires that such premises are at least adequately fit for human habitation at the beginning or presentation of tenancy; see further *Siney* v *Dublin Corporation* [1980] IR 400.

This implication that the landlord is under a duty to have certain basic standards as regards a furnished house can be traced in a statutory sense to Section 114 of the Housing Act 1966. These provisions were strengthened by the Housing (Standards for Rented Houses) Regulations 1993 (SI 1993/147), made pursuant to the Housing Act 1992, which came into operation for private rented accommodation on 1 January 1994 and for local authority housing on 1 January 1998. These regulations require landlords to ensure that the accommodation meets certain minimum requirements as regards heating, lighting and ventilation. Article 5 of the regulations specifically requires landlords to keep the property in a proper state of structural repair.

Tenant

As regards the tenant, his obligations will typically be comprehensively governed by the terms of the repair and maintain covenant in the lease. In the absence of an express term, the tenant is obliged to keep the premises in a 'tenant-like manner' or, as stated in *Warren* v *Keen* [1954] 1 QB 15, 'wind and watertight, fair wear and tear excepted'.

This obligation of the tenant is also highlighted by Section 42 of Deasy's Act. Section 42 implies that the tenant will return the premises in good and substantial repair and condition on determination of the lease. It must be stressed that both the common law obligations and Section 42 only apply if there is no express 'repair and maintain' covenant in the lease.

There are certain qualifications to the duty of the tenant to repair and maintain the premises. For example, if the property is accidentally destroyed in part by fire then the tenant is under no duty to repair such damage as is physically impossible or financially exorbitant to rectify and he may return, or in more legal terms, surrender, his tenancy without liability. This exception is detailed in Section 40 of Deasy's Act and it is strengthened by Section 65 of the Landlord and Tenant (Amendment) Act 1980, which states that the principle applies to the benefit of the tenant regardless of any express covenant to the contrary. Section 65 states that the landlord is only entitled to recover damages for that which is lost in the value of the premises due to the wilfully reckless behaviour of the tenant; see further *Gilligan* v *Silke* [1963] IR 1, a case considered under the old Section 55 of the Landlord and Tenant Act 1931 (in effect restated by Section 65).

Apart from the covenant to repair and maintain the property, other important clauses or covenants that would be included in the typical lease agreement would be rent and assignment clauses, as well as a user clause.

Rent

Invariably, the primary covenant undertaken by the tenant is to pay a specified rent at an appointed, regular interval and often in advance. The tenant may also be responsible for paying rates and other overheads like gas, electricity and telephone. Interesting statutory additions to this area are the Housing (Rent Books) Regulations 1993 (SI 1993/146) made pursuant to the Housing Act 1992, which came into operation for private rented accommodation on 1 September 1993. Each new tenant must be supplied with a rent book containing basic information about the rent, primarily its method and frequency of payment.

Assignment

At common law, an assignment of a tenancy may involve the out and out transfer of the entire tenant's interest so that he retains nothing and the assignee succeeds to his rights and duties. Given the extent of this power of assignment vested in the tenant it is usual to insert in the lease agreement a covenant expressly requiring the tenant to give written notification to the landlord of an intention to assign in order to obtain the landlord's consent to the assignment; see Section 66 of the Landlord and Tenant (Amendment) Act 1980.

The consent must not be unreasonably withheld by the landlord; see further *Crowe Ltd* v *Dublin Port and Docks Ltd* [1962] IR 194, *OHS Ltd* v *Green Property Co. Ltd* [1986] IR 39 and *Schlegel* v *Corcoran* [1942] IR 19.

Use of the property

In the case of a residential premises there is usually a covenant or agreement by the tenant requiring him to use the premises as a private dwelling house only and not to use it for the purposes of carrying out any business, trade or profession. Equally, the business tenant may be covenanted to use the premises for specific commercial use only, although the use of the premises for another kind of trade or business may not necessarily be a breach of the covenant unless it is clearly 'offensive' to the agreement; see further *Byrne v Fox* [1938] IR 683.

The general principle behind such covenants is that the landlord is trying to protect his interest. The property will eventually return to the landlord and he may not want its value reduced by the use made of it by the tenant in the meantime; see further *O'Gorman v Dublin Corporation* [1949] IR 40 and *Crowe Ltd v Dublin Port and Docks Board* [1962] IR 294.

Statutory control of tenancies

The Landlord and Tenant (Amendment) Act 1980 (effective from 8 September 1980) and the Landlord and Tenant (Amendment) Act 1994 (effective from 10 August 1994) assist in the regulation of the relationship between landlord and tenant by providing a number of statutory reliefs to the parties in question. Arguably, the recent legislation assists in redressing the balance that traditionally favoured the landlord in the tenancy relationship. As an example, the Landlord and Tenant (Amendment) Act 1980 gives tenants two significant statutory rights. First, there is the right to compensation for improvements and the second right concerns the capacity of the tenant to renew a tenancy.

Before detailed mention is made of these rights there is a need to make two introductory remarks.

First, the 1980 Act concerns itself with what it calls *tenements*. Section 5(1) of the Act states that for the purposes of the Act, a tenement means premises that consist either of land covered wholly or partly by buildings or of a defined portion of a building. Section 5(1) goes on to state that where the premises consist of land covered in part only by buildings, the portion of land not so covered is also included under the terms of the Act where it can be deemed subsidiary and ancillary to the buildings.

In general the courts take a pretty liberal view of the definition of a building; see further *Dursley v Watters* [1993] 1 IR 224 and *Terry v Stokes* [1993] 1 IR 204, where self-assembled sheds were deemed to come under the definition of a building given in Section 5. In *Kenny v Leonard*, 11 December 1997, High Court, Costello, P., held that a car park was not ancillary to a small office that received parking fees and keys, though it was accepted that the office was ancillary to the business of parking cars. Similarly, it was accepted that underground petrol storage tanks were buildings within the meaning of the 1980 Act and that the area of land over the tanks was ancillary to the filling station business.

Secondly, apart from the vital definition of a tenement, there is another distinction that has to be made in discussing the scheme of the 1980 Act. It is necessary to distinguish between business tenancies — a commercial operation; and occupational tenancies — residential premises. This distinction is necessary as the 1980 Act may differently affect both types of tenancies.

Alterations and improvements

Compensation for improvements is available to both business and residential tenants. Part IV of the 1980 Act, which includes Sections 45–63, governs this area of the law. Section 45 of the 1980 Act defines an improvement to a tenement as 'any addition or alteration of the building ... but does not include work consisting only of repairing, painting and decorating, or any of them.' Section 46 provides that where a tenant quits a tenement on legal termination of his tenancy, he is entitled to be paid, by the landlord, compensation for every improvement made on the tenement that adds to the letting value of the property. If the landlord and tenant cannot agree a sum in compensation then application can be made to the courts under Section 47 of the 1980 Act. In deciding the amount of compensation that may be payable the courts should have regard to the probable durability of the improvement.

However, to be able to take advantage of the Act, the tenant must serve, as per Sections 48 to 55 of the 1980 Act, a notice of intention to execute the improvement in question. This notice must include giving details of the work and estimates of its cost. If the landlord does not object within one month he is deemed to have consented to the outlined changes. In fact, during this one-month period the landlord has three options:

- He may simply consent to the improvement serving what the 1980 Act calls an *improvement* notice.
- He may serve an *improvement undertaking* agreeing to do the work himself and asking for an increased rent in the future. (Most professional landlords will do this to guarantee work standards).
- He may object to the improvement by serving an *improvement objection*.

In the case of consent, the tenant has one year in which to execute the improvement; see further Section 50 of the 1980 Act. In the case of an improvement undertaking by the landlord, the tenant can object to the increased rent and bring an action in the Circuit Court to determine the new rent or to deal with the matter as an improvement objection; see further Section 51. In the case of an outright objection by the landlord, the tenant can again bring an action to the Circuit Court or simply resign himself to withdrawing the notice for improvement; see further Section 52.

Finally, where an improvement is carried out by the tenant then, under Section 55, the landlord must issue, if asked, an improvement certificate certifying that the improvement has been made in accordance with the notice or order. This will assist the tenant in case the landlord or a successor challenges the improvement at a later time.

Right of renewal

Part II (Sections 13–29) of the 1980 Act governs the right to a new tenancy. Part II of the 1980 Act gives tenants the right to a new tenancy on satisfaction of certain conditions.

As regards business tenants, under Section 13(1)(a) of the 1980 Act the right to a new tenancy was originally given to all business tenants of three years' standing, that is, if the tenants have been in continuous occupation of the premises for three years. This was amended to five years by Section 3 of the 1994 Act. As regards a residential tenant, the tenant may base his claim in equity on the basis of 'long occupation'. Section 13(1)(b) of the 1980 Act defines long occupation as 20 years. Both a business and residential tenant can make use of Section 13(1)(c) which permits new tenancy rights on 'extensive improvement', which is deemed to be more than half the letting value of the tenement.

It must be noted that as regards business tenants, Section 13(2) of the 1980 Act states that a 'temporary break in the use' of a business tenement can be disregarded if the court considers it reasonable to do so. It appears from the case law that while there may be a break in the use of the business tenement the lessee must at all times remain a valid tenant of the premises and not, for example, a caretaker of the premises; see further *Gatien Motor Co. Ltd v Continental Oil Co. of Ireland* [1979] IR 406, as governed by the Landlord and Tenant Act 1931.

Terms of new tenancy

Section 16 provides that where a tenant complies with Part II of the 1980 Act, he is entitled to a new tenancy commencing on the termination of his previous tenancy. The terms of this new tenancy may be agreed by the landlord and tenant or, in the absence of same, Section 18 states that the terms can be fixed by the court. Under Section 23 of the 1980 Act the court must fix the duration of the tenancy at 35 years or such lesser term as the tenant may nominate.

The practical application of Section 23 proved unsatisfactory for landlords. Under Section 23, a tenant could seek a new tenancy for a very short time period, for example, one year, at the end of which he would in all likelihood be entitled to seek a further renewal from the court. This practice of short-term renewal deprived landlords of secure and predictable income from premises, with, in particular, consequent financial implications for the management of commercial investment properties. Section 5 of the 1994 Act amended Section 23 of the 1980 Act to the extent that where the right to renew a tenancy is based on a business tenancy (as per Section 13(1)(a) of the 1980 Act) the duration of the tenancy will be fixed at 20 years or such lesser term as the tenant may nominate; but it will not be fixed for a period of less than five years without the landlord's agreement.

Section 23 of the 1980 Act also details the rent that can be set by the court for the new tenancy. As per Section 23(5), the rent set is the 'gross rent' reduced, if appropriate, by an allowance for improvements. Gross rent is essentially the rent the property would obtain if it were let on the open market. The court cannot fix a rent review clause in such a lease but both the landlord and tenant are entitled to apply to the court for a review of the rent at five yearly intervals. Under Section 15 of the Landlord and Tenant (Amendment) Act 1984, the party seeking the rent review must serve one month's notice on the other party for the first review.

Finally, the prescribed forms for claiming a new tenancy are set out in the Landlord and Tenant Regulations 1980 (SI 1980/272).

Restrictions

Section 17 of the 1980 Act outlines various circumstances in which the tenant may be disentitled to a renewal of tenancy. For example, under Section 17(1) the tenant has no right to a new tenancy if the existing one is terminated by ejectment for non-payment of rent or for breach of a covenant by the tenant or by the tenant's surrender of the tenancy or if the landlord has given notice to quit to the tenant on good and sufficient reason.

Section 17(2) also outlines instances where a tenant may not be entitled to a new tenancy. These are more technical reasons and are to do with necessary reconstruction or redevelopment of the property. In such examples the fact that the tenant is not entitled to a new tenancy is through no fault of his own and thus he shall be entitled to compensation for disturbance, see for example *Ryan* v *Bradley* [1956] IR 31 which concerns itself with the predecessor of Section 17, Section 22 of the Landlord and Tenant Act 1931.

Finally, a tenant of an office premises can waive his right of renewal under Section 4 of the 1994 Act but can only do so after obtaining independent legal advice.

Enforcement of obligations

The remedies available to the landlord and tenant for the enforcement of their respective obligations depend partly on the terms of the tenancy agreement and partly on general law, that is, common law and statute.

Action

As there is privity of contract between the parties to the lease agreement they may sue each other in contract for breach of any of the terms of the lease. In addition to this common law right of action, the landlord has a statutory right, under Section 45 of Deasy's Act, to sue for rent in arrears, though Section 48 of the same Act states that the tenant may make a reduction on same in respect of 'all just debts' due to him from the landlord; the landlord may therefore be estopped from recovering the full rent if the tenant has completed an agreed condition to so reduce the rent.

Distress

At common law the landlord had a traditional right, if the tenant failed to perform his obligations, to enter the premises and seize the chattels of the tenant and hold them as a pledge until the tenant performed his obligations. Over the years many restrictions on the remedy of distress have developed, particularly in statute. For example, under Section 51 of Deasy's Act no distress can be taken for rent due more than a year before the distress and, under the Law of Distress and Small Debts (Ireland) Act 1888, various goods, usually highly personal ones, are protected or exempt from distress. If a wrongful distress is made, a tenant may seek damages or an injunction to prevent against the loss of the goods; see further *Re Cassidy* [1904] IR 427. In Northern Ireland this rather dubious and draconian measure was abolished by the Judgements Enforcement Act (Northern Ireland) 1969 and in the Republic it is highly unlikely that distress would be seen to be consistent with the proprietary rights enshrined in our Constitution.

Successors in title

It is important to remember that in landlord and tenant law obligations may be enforceable by and against not only the original parties to the tenancy agreement but also their successors in title. This principle has been given statutory recognition by Sections 12 and 13 of Deasy's Act; see further *Lyle* v *Smith* [1909] 2 IR 58.

Determination of the relationship of landlord and tenant

The principal ways in which the relationship of landlord and tenant may determine are outlined below.

Expiry

If, for example, one has a tenancy for a fixed period of one year, the most obvious way in which the tenancy expires is at the end of that year. In the circumstances of a term certain no notice to quit is required.

Surrender

Under Section 7 of Deasy's Act a tenant can surrender the tenancy to the landlord by deed or writing. Surrender may also be inferred from the acts of the parties, for example, handing back the key; see further *Lynch* v *Lynch* (1843) 6 Ir L R 131.

Forfeiture and ejectment

At common law the landlord can re-enter the property for breach of a condition of the agreement by the tenant. In this instance the tenant is said to have forfeited the lease or tenancy agreement and is duly ejected. It seems that for an effective forfeiture to occur the landlord must actually and physically enter the property and retake possession of the property; see further O'Hanlon, J., in *Bank of Ireland* v *Lady Lisa Ireland Ltd* [1992] 1 IR 404. Forfeiture or re-entry for breach of a condition or covenant is still largely governed by the Conveyancing Acts 1881 and 1892. Section 14(1) of the 1881 Act stresses that in such proceedings sufficient and clear notice of re-entry must be given; see further *Breadan* v *Fuller* [1949] IR 290, *MCB* v *IDA* [1981] ILRM 58, *O'Connor* v *Mooney* [1982] ILRM 373 and *Enock* v *Jones Estates Ltd* [1983] ILRM 532.

In the case of non-payment of rent the landlord usually invokes the statutory remedy of ejectment; see further Section 52 of Deasy's Act.

Notice to quit

If the tenancy is periodic rather than fixed then a notice to quit may be served. It is important to note that the landlord is entitled to determine the periodic tenancy for no given reason. The tenant does not have to be in breach and the motive of the landlord is irrelevant. Though the landlord's right is absolute, the tenant may have certain rights to renew the lease under the 1980 Act. It seems that under Section 16 of the Housing Act 1992 the notice to quit will not be valid unless it is in writing and is served not less than four weeks before the date on which it is to take effect. Notice must expire on a *gale day*, that is, a day on which a periodic payment of rent is due.

For a weekly tenancy, the statutory minimum of four weeks' notice is required. At common law, a monthly tenancy requires one month's notice expiring on a gale day. Three months' notice, expiring on a gale day, suffices for a quarterly tenancy; while a tenancy on a year-to-year basis requires six months (a full 183 days), expiring on the anniversary of the date of commencement of the tenancy. If the date of commencement is unknown, as per Section 6 of Deasy's Act it will be presumed to have begun on the last gale day of the year on which the rent has become due. Normally, there are four gale days in each year for the payment of yearly rents and traditionally these days were based on religious feasts, for example, 25 March (Annunciation), 29 June (St James and St John), 29 September (St Michael) and 25 December (the Nativity).

New developments

The insecurity of tenure associated with this last issue of notice highlights that in Ireland the issue of tenants' rights is in need of further consideration. This is particularly clear if we compare the legal status of Irish private residential tenancies to that of our European counterparts. It is noted that on 5 January 2001, the Minister for Housing and Urban Renewal, announced a government proposal for major reform in the private rented residential sector arising from the recommendations in the report of the Commission on the Private Rented Residential Sector. The major reforms proposed are the establishment by autumn 2001 of an informal, ad hoc Private Residential Tenancies Board (PRTB) to deal primarily with disputes between landlords and tenants and the enactment within a two-year time frame of legislation to provide for the establishment of the PRTB on a statutory basis, improved security of tenure mechanisms, graduated notice to quit periods and also certain rent controls.

As regards the security of tenure issue, legislation is to be enacted to grant private residential tenants, whose tenancy has not been terminated in the first six months and who comply with the obligations relating to the tenancy, a right to continue in occupation for the remainder of a four-year period, unless the landlord needs to recover possession for specified reasons. These reasons are that the accommodation is no longer suitable for the tenant's circumstances by reference to the number of bed spaces and/or the landlord wishes to sell or substantially refurbish/renovate the property in a way which requires the property to be vacated, or to change its business use, or requires it for his own or family member occupation. Successive four-year tenancy periods are envisaged, incorporating at the outset a six-month period during which the landlord may terminate the tenancy without one of the specified grounds being applicable.

As regards the graduated notice to quit periods, it is proposed that unless the tenancy is being terminated for failure to comply with its obligations, a graduated notice period will apply related to the length of the tenancy in each four-year period. Notice to quit requirements will range from a minimum of four weeks (28 days) to a maximum of 16 weeks (112 days).

As regards rent levels, it is proposed that rents may be no greater than the market rate and reviews may occur no more frequently than once a year (unless there is a substantial change to the nature of the accommodation before the review date).

Leases and licences

Currently, a tenant under a lease agreement has a number of substantial rights, as assisted in particular by statutory developments. In a general sense, the tenant has a certain amount of security of tenure. He is free to assign his rights and duties and also has increasing statutory rights wherein he may qualify for the right to compensation for disturbance and improvements and even the right to a renewal of tenancy. Landlords have long since attempted to evade such protections by labelling tenancies *licences*, where a licence is defined as merely a permission to do an act which otherwise would be unlawful. In other words, a licence falls short of giving a sufficient proprietary interest in the land to constitute a lease. In fact, the security of the licensee is of little value; the landlord can transfer his interest without reference to the licence; a licence cannot be assigned nor are the statutory protections given to tenants available to the licensee.

In short, a licence has a more personal element to it than a lease or tenancy agreement. It follows that the significance of distinguishing between a lease and a licence is the related rights that attach to each. At its most basic, if the agreement with the property owner can be described as a lease, the occupier will have considerably more rights, not only at common law but also at statutory level. Before we discuss the manner in which the courts distinguish between a lease and a licence, a few examples of what is said to constitute a licence are necessary. They include such diverse scenarios as the permission of usage in hiring a hall for several days, house rights to sell refreshments at a concert, or even permission to erect advertising hoarding on land bordering a main road.

Lease v licence: how the courts decide

Lord Denning, M.R., remarked in *Shell-Mex* v *Manchester Garages* [1971] 1 WLR 612, p. 615, that the courts are well aware that:

> Although a document may be described as a licence, it does not necessarily follow that, merely on that account, it is to be regarded as amounting only to a licence in law. Whether the transaction is a licence or a tenancy does not depend on the label that is put on it. It depends on the nature of the transaction itself. Broadly speaking, we have to see whether it is a personal privilege given to a person (in which case it is a licence) or whether it grants an interest in land (in which case it is a tenancy).

Lord Denning's remarks, which are helpful in summary, were cited with approval in Ireland in cases such as *Gatien Motor Co.* v *Continental Oil* [1979] IR 406 and *Irish Shell* v *Costello* (No. 1) [1981] ILRM 66. They are also interesting in that his Lordship, while observing that the test is now a broad one based on whether the agreement is personal in nature, admitted that at one time it used to be thought that exclusive possession was a decisive factor. Indeed, evidence of exclusive possession still plays a large role in the distinction between a lease and a licence.

Exclusive possession

Exclusive possession means that on upholding the terms of the agreement the occupant has the right to exclude the owner from the premises for the duration of the agreement. This right to exclusive possession is an essential part of a lease or tenancy but not of a licence. Traditionally, judges were prone to remarking that the presence of exclusive possession negatives a licence; see further *Lynes* v *Snaith* [1895–9] All ER Rep 997. Now the matter is subtler and exclusive possession is merely one of the factors, although, as we shall see, along with the payment of rent it is the most important factor, that the court takes into account as distinguishing between a lease and a licence.

This relegation of the importance of exclusive possession as a factor can be traced back to a series of decisions in England in the 1950s beginning with *Errington* v *Errington* [1952] 1 All ER 149 and continuing with *Cobb* v *Lane* [1952] 1 All ER 1199. In the latter case, Roskill, L.J., referred to the fact that exclusive occupation of the property for an indefinite period was no longer inconsistent with the occupier being deemed a licensee. It was argued that whether the relationship of landlord and tenant had been created depended on the intention and conduct of the parties involved, that is, whether the agreement was personal in nature (licence) or gave an interest in the land (lease).

This reasoning was later cited with approval by Scarman, L.J., in *Heslop* v *Burns* [1974] 3 All ER 406 and followed more immediately by the influential case of *Addiscombe Garden Estates* v *Crabbe* [1958] 1 QB 513. In *Addiscombe*, exclusive possession was treated as merely one of the factors the court had to take into account in deciding whether the parties intended by their conduct to create a lease or a licence. This approach is often known as the *balance sheet approach.*

In *Addiscombe*, the occupant was a tennis club that sought to stay on at the end of the agreed period. If, as they argued, they had a lease, it gave them the statutory right to security of tenure; however, it was contested that the interest they had was merely a licence. The court held that while the agreement described itself as a licence the label could not be taken as conclusive and the court preferred to look at the actual intention of the parties, that is, the substance of the agreement, not the form. In doing so the court adopted the aforementioned balance sheet approach of which exclusive possession was merely one factor.

The court took into account that as the document required the occupant to keep the premises in good repair this implied a lease. The agreement also prevented the occupant tennis club from cutting down trees on the premises. The court took into account the fact that, if the agreement was merely a licence, the owner would not have felt the need to include such a clause, therefore its inclusion indicated a strong proprietary interest being given to the occupant implying a lease. Similarly, the owner expressly reserved the right to enter the premises for inspection. Implicitly, the court argued, this indicated that the owner was recognising the occupants' exclusive possession of the land for the fixed period. Finally, the court noted that rent was payable, thus indicating a lease.

On balance, the court felt that the agreement constituted a lease.

This balance sheet approach, of which exclusive possession was but one of the factors, reached its zenith in the aforementioned case of *Shell-Mex* v *Manchester Garages Ltd* [1971] 1 WLR 612, where the plaintiffs owned a petrol station and had a licence with the defendants which allowed the defendants to use the pumps and the premises. The agreed time period ran out and the defendants argued that the agreement was in fact a lease entitling them to greater statutory protection.

The court applied the balance sheet approach and noted immediately the fact that the word 'licence' was specifically used in the agreement. Even though this was only a label and not therefore conclusive, it was a factor to be considered. Second, there was in the view of the court a personal element to the agreement in that the defendants were only to sell the plaintiff's petrol and indeed would receive a reward or bonus the more they sold. Third, it seemed from the agreement that there was no exclusive possession and that this indicated, although not conclusively so, that a mere licence existed. The balance thus favoured the creation of a licence with the court noting that the nature of the transaction, particularly the personal element to it, indicated that the intention was to create the relationship of licensee and licensor.

The problem with this approach is that it overly favours the owner in that he can avoid the statutory obligations of a landlord by couching the agreement in the terms of a licence, as highlighted by the case of *Somme* v *Hazelhurst* [1978] 2 All ER 1011. The decision to describe the agreement as a licence permitted the owner to avoid the application of the relevant Rent Acts. It is possible that with this in mind Lord Templeman in *Street* v *Mountford* [1985] 2 All ER 289 chose to tighten up this area of the law.

Lord Templeman leaned against the balance sheet approach, arguing that if the occupier had exclusive possession of the premises for a fixed or periodic term at rent, a tenancy was to be presumed and expressions of intentions otherwise were irrelevant. In the immediate case the landlord granted the appellant the right to occupy a furnished room under a written agreement which stated that the appellant had the right to occupy the room 'at a licence fee of £37 a week', that 'this personal licence is not assignable', that the licence 'may be terminated by 14 days written notice' and that the appellant understood and accepted that a 'licence in the above form does not and is not intended to give me a tenancy protected under the Rents Acts'. The appellant had exclusive possession of the room. Some months after signing the agreement the appellant applied to have a fair rent registered in respect of the room. The landlord then applied to the court for a declaration that the appellant occupied the room under a licence not a tenancy.

Lord Templeman forwarded the view that, regardless of the label given to the agreement, if the agreement satisfied all the requirements of a tenancy — exclusive possession for term at rent (which was the case here) — then the agreement was presumed to produce a tenancy and no amount of labelling could make it otherwise. As his Lordship eloquently put it:

> The manufacture of a five-pronged implement for manual digging results in a fork even if the manufacturer, unfamiliar with the English language, insists that he intended to make and has made a spade.

Accordingly, since the effect of the agreement between the appellant and the landlord was to grant the appellant exclusive possession for a fixed term at a stated rent, and no circumstances existed to negative the presumption of a tenancy, it was clear that the appellant was a tenant. The appeal was therefore allowed.

It has been argued that in apparently shifting the emphasis back onto exclusive possession that the English House of Lords in that case effected a radical change in the law. Admittedly, the House of Lords in Street v Mountford did tighten up the previous balance sheet approach and restored primacy to the issues of exclusive possession and rent, but to say that the approach therein was a radical one is false for a number of reasons.

First, in the course of judgements given, the reasoning of Denning in *Errington* and *Addiscombe* was expressly affirmed. Second, Lord Templeman acknowledged that while exclusive possession for a term at rent did give rise to a presumption of a tenancy, like all presumptions it could be rebutted on further evidence. Third, in this particular case the House of Lords was anxious to ensure that landlords who attempted to avoid their statutory obligations would not be facilitated by describing the agreement in question as a licence and the court should be astute enough to recognise and frustrate such artificial transactions.

Lease v licence: the Irish view

In *Gatien Motor Co. Ltd* v *Continental Oil* [1979] IR 406, the Supreme Court considered and agreed with the leading English authorities preceding *Street* v *Mountford*. The Supreme Court seemed to favour the balance sheet approach in which exclusive possession, while a factor in indicating a tenancy, was not conclusive evidence of same. In *Gatien* the occupier had a three-year tenancy and the owner wished to avoid the statutory rights — for example, the right to a new tenancy — which the occupier would receive if the agreement lasted the full three-year tenancy. To this end, the owner made a special caretaker agreement with the occupier for two weeks during which the occupier did not pay rent. The owner then proceeded to grant a new three-year tenancy to the occupier.

When the first three-year period ended the occupier tried to claim his statutory rights and the key question was whether the two-week caretaker period was a lease or a licence. If it was a licence then the three-year original tenancy was broken and the statutory rights of the tenant would go with it. The court held that it was a licence implying that the occupier lost his statutory rights, adopting the balance sheet approach but giving priority to the presence or otherwise of exclusive possession and rent. The court held that while exclusive possession remained active during the two-week period, both parties had independent legal advice and were deemed well aware of the scheme behind the temporary caretaker agreement. The court also took into account the fact that during the two weeks no rent was paid. These factors led it to conclude that a licence existed.

A similar broad approach placing factors such as exclusive possession and rent at the top of the balance sheet was followed in the Supreme Court decision of *Irish Shell* v *Costello* (No. 1) [1981] ILRM 66 where the court had to determine the effect of a written agreement whereby the defendants had been given the right to use a petrol station owned by the plaintiffs. The agreement purported to authorise the defendants to use the land only for this specific service, using equipment (petrol pumps, etc.) supplied by the plaintiffs. Periodic payments were said to arise from the 'hire' of this equipment.

Griffin, J., and O'Higgins, J., agreed that the landlord and tenant relationship had been created and went on to identify a number of factors as being indicative of the true nature of the relationship between the parties. They rated as most important the fact that the documents forwarded in evidence demonstrated that it was intended that the defendants should have the exclusive right to occupy the premises. These documents showed the owner expressly reserving the right to inspect the premises from time to time; the court took this as the owner implicitly acknowledging that the occupier had exclusive possession. The court in interpreting the prohibition on the occupier from assignment used similar 'converse' reasoning. Finally, Griffin, J., in particular, regarded the periodic payment for the hire of the equipment as being equivalent to rent and, given these factors, it was held that a lease existed.

It is interesting to note that Kenny, J., dissented vigorously and while he acknowledged the element of exclusive possession, he argued that no express rent was paid and the personal nature of the agreement (the occupier could only sell the owner's petrol) indicated the intention to create a licence only. In *Irish Shell v Costello* (No. 2) [1984] IR 511, a case which followed the ending of the original tenancy, the agreement was held by the majority in the Supreme Court to be a licence. While the occupiers remained in exclusive possession and paid a rent, this arrangement was qualified by the fact that it was acknowledged to be only a tentative interim payment pending further negotiations. Thus, the occupiers were now deemed licensees.

In sum, the approach of the Irish courts seems to be equivalent to that of the broad balance sheet approach favoured by the English courts prior to *Street v Mountford*; see further *Bellew v Bellew* [1982] IR 447, where the occupiers were clearly in exclusive possession, but other factors — in *Bellew*, the personal element of the relationship — led to the court holding that only a licence had in fact been given. However, it is argued that the Irish approach is a little subtler than the rather scattered balance sheet approach of earlier English cases. It is submitted that the Irish approach is closer to Lord Templeman's approach in *Street v Mountford* than would appear at first glance.

The approach of the Irish courts is a balance sheet approach but at the top of that list they invariably place the Templeman factors of exclusive possession for term at rent. If these factors are present, there is a presumption of tenancy that is difficult to rebut; see *Irish Shell* (No. 1). But, arguably more so than Lord Templeman, the Irish courts acknowledge that that presumption can be rebutted notably by factors such as the highly personal element to the agreement (*Bellew*) or the fact that both sides had legal advice as regards the nature of the agreement (*Gatien Motor*) or that the conduct of the parties suggested otherwise (*Irish Shell* (No. 2)).

Further reading

Brennan, G., (ed.) *Law Society of Ireland: Landlord and Tenant Law*. London: Blackstone Press, 2000.

Coughlan, P., *Property Law*, 2nd edn. Dublin: Gill & MacMillan, 1998, Chapters 15 and 16.

Lyall, A., *Land Law in Ireland*, 2nd edn. Dublin: Round Hall Sweet & Maxwell, 2000, Chapter 19.

Wylie, J., *Irish Land Law*, 3rd edn. Dublin: Butterworths, 1997, Chapters 17 and 18.

Wylie, J., *Irish Landlord and Tenant Law*, 2nd edn. Dublin: Butterworths, 1998.

Self-test

1. John O'Shaughnessy is the owner of premises at 13 Infirmary Road, Dublin, in which he resided until 1995 when he retired to live in Leitrim. In 1995 he signed a letting agreement with a young doctor, Dr H. Lecter, under which Dr Lecter would use the premises for the purposes of his medical surgery at an agreed rent for a term of one year. Other yearly agreements were executed annually each year from 1996–2000.

    In 1996, Mr O'Shaughnessy allowed Dr Lecter to reside with his family on the premises and the rent was increased as a result. Dr Lecter carried on a very successful practice on the premises, despite an occasional smell, although he was absent for a period of six months in 1996 when he went to a remote part of Indonesia on a lecture tour. Nevertheless, the Lecter family continued to live in the premises during that period. When he got back from Indonesia, Lecter arranged, with the consent of the landlord, to have an extension, including a patio, built on to the surgery and to have the entire premises re-wired.

    The latest agreement is due to expire shortly and Mr O'Shaughnessy now wants vacant possession. As his legal counsel Dr Lecter has invited you for lunch. What will you advise him?

Key points

Answer the question in the light of the rights given to the tenant under the Landlord and Tenant (Amendment) 1980. Is it a tenement for the purposes of the Act? Is it a business or residential tenancy?

Irrespective of what type of tenancy it is, Dr Lecter may be entitled to compensation for the significant improvements made to the property as per sections 48–55 of the 1980 Act. Indeed, such are the extent of the improvements, would Dr Lecter have a case, under Section 13(1)(c) of the 1980 Act, to a renewal of the tenancy? If Dr Lecter is a business tenant he must establish five years' continuous occupation before he can apply for a renewal of tenancy under Section 13(1)(a) of the 1980 Act. Was he in continuous occupation for a five-year period? Even if Dr Lecter qualifies for a renewal under Section 13, as per Section 17(1) of the 1980 Act, Dr Lecter may be disentitled to a renewal and as per Section 17(2) Mr O'Shaugnessy may not be obliged to renew the tenancy. In addition, are similar considerations to be taken into account for the renewal of a residential tenancy under the 1980 Act? Finally, is notice to quit required?

2. Statol is a Scandinavian oil company. They enter into an agreement with Terry Blair whereby Terry will run a petrol station for them in Nenagh. The agreement describes itself as a licence. Terry is to sell Statol petrol only. There is a provision in the agreement allowing representatives of Statol to come onto the premises once a month to make sure that safety measures are being adhered to and that customers are being treated with suitable politeness. There is no rent payable but Terry is to pay 1,000 a month for hire of the petrol pumps. He is prohibited from assigning his interest.

Discuss the interest that Terry has received from Statol.

Key points

The key issue here is whether Terry has received a lease, which may guarantee him certain statutory protections; or has he received a mere licence? In distinguishing between a lease and a licence, note the following:

•   The facts are set in Ireland, therefore English case law is persuasive only. The scenario is also set in a petrol station, therefore cases such as *Shell-Mex* (Eng) and the *Irish Shell cases* (Ire) are relevant.

- The agreement describes itself as a licence. Is labelling sufficient of itself? Generally the courts say no and they look to the substance rather than the form; see Lord Templeman's quote regarding the five-prong fork in *Street v Mountford*. Nevertheless, labelling may be of assistance as per Lord Denning in *Shell-Mex*.
- Terry is to sell Statol petrol only. This implies a personal element to the agreement, which would hint at a licence as per *Shell-Mex*, *Irish Shell* (No. 2) and *Bellew v Bellew*. However, in *Irish Shell* (No 1) this personal element was overridden by the presence of exclusive possession and the payment of rent.
- Statol retain the right to inspect the premises. If Terry has a licence there would be no need to reserve this right. Therefore, as per *Addiscombe* and *Irish Shell* (No. 1), this is a good and converse indication of a lease. Similar reasoning can be applied to the prohibition on the assignment. Again, this is a converse indication of a lease.
- No express rent is paid but 'hire' on pumps is equivalent to rent as per the majority in *Irish Shell* (No. 1).
- On balance Terry seems to have exclusive possession and he pays rent, therefore there is a presumption of a tenancy as per Templeman, L.J., in *Street v Mountford*. But in Ireland the courts would be more willing to admit evidence to rebut this presumption; for example: What was the intention of the parties as expressed in the agreement? Did their conduct suggest the presumption of a lease or otherwise? Can the presumption of a tenancy be defeated on the grounds that Terry has received independent legal advice as to the nature of the agreement? If the agreement is deemed a licence, will this help Statol evade certain statutory duties as per *Somme v Hazelhurst*, and should this be permitted?